More Than All The Steps

Nicholas H. Lang

More Than All The Steps
Nicholas H. Lang

© 2020 by Nicholas H. Lang
All rights reserved.

Edited by Adam Colwell's WriteWorks, LLC: Adam Colwell and Ginger Colwell
Cover concept and design: Boundless Design: Joshua White
Interior design and typesetting: New Herald Publishing: Shua Miller
Published by New Herald Publishing

Printed in the United States of America
ISBN (Paperback):
ISBN (eBook):

*To my wife, Hannah, who is the most loving human being
I have ever known.*

SAINT JAMES IS BURIED IN THE CATHEDRAL OF SANTIAGO, SPAIN.

Or at least that's what they say.

There's a huge story behind how James' body ended up there, complete with a shipwreck and a few miracles. Part of the legend has his body buried and lost until God led someone to the exact spot to dig it back up and bring it to Santiago.

The truth of the stories varies depending on who you talk to—and I wonder if it really matters at all, because the reason most people journey to the cathedral to honor the venerable saint and his old bones is to walk.

It's called the Camino de Santiago, or the Way of Saint James. I first heard about it from my wife, Hannah, after she watched a movie featuring people who had traversed it. When we got married, one of the things that we promised each other was to continue to adventure and travel the world. We've shot down into Mexico a few times, which is pretty easy since we live about an hour from the border in Tucson, Arizona. Malawi, Africa, has been a repeated missions trip for us. We've been on safari in nearby Zambia. We've cruised the Caribbean and have even hiked through Nepal for 19 days. So, when Hannah told me about the Camino de Santiago, which starts at the French border and runs through Spain, I knew we had to do it. It would be a chance to see the

Spanish countryside in a way you simply can't in a car or on a train. To go slowly and see the terrain and architecture, from the rocks and crevices to the minute cracks in the cathedrals along the way.

The pilgrim taking the Way of Saint James is supposed to be someone in search of some sort of significant spiritual experience. Yet many of the people in the documentary, and most of the people we encountered on the journey, really weren't looking for anything supernatural. They just seemed to find their way to it through a variety of circumstances. One man, whose life was so stressful he was literally going blind, told me he needed to refresh. Another girl lost her job and her boyfriend the same day, and with her apartment lease getting ready to end, she just up and left. She needed to reassess. A third young man was straight out of the military and needed to rediscover himself after doing only what others had told him to do for so long.

Hannah and I simply saw it as an adventure waiting to be had, though our own spiritual backgrounds each came into play in our decision to walk the Camino. By the time we left for France, I was 30 and had been a pastor for six years. My motivation was two-fold. First, I love Christian tradition and knew the sites along the route would offer me the opportunity to experience the richness of centuries-old history and the origins of theology. I also love to be outdoors, and I saw hiking as a way to clear my head and enjoy creation. It is a space where I can just be me, push myself physically, sing, be silent, and pray. Basically, it is a place of freedom. I was definitely in for 30 days of hiking.

My wife, on the other hand, wanted to get away and journey with Jesus. She looked at the Camino as a prayer walk. She saw herself walking with God and connecting with Him in ways that she never had, a time where she could press in to her relationship with the Lord. I think part of her motivation, too, was to prove to herself that she had it in her. Trekking 500 miles with a heavy backpack was something bigger and more challenging than anything she had done. If she could complete this and do it well, she could do anything. She'd always tell me, "I just want to prove to myself that I can do hard things."

A few months before we hit the trail, I received some unexpected news. I was told that I needed a knee replacement. It stemmed from a rock-climbing injury in my teenage years where I fell 50 feet and completely wrecked my left knee and ankle. Suddenly, I had to make a decision. Do I cancel the trip and get surgery, or slap on a brace and tough it out? My doc kept pushing and telling me there was no way that I could make a 500-mile walk with a bum knee, but all I could think about was the fact that I was 30 years old. How many people my age actually need knee replacements? It's way too young.

Toughing it out seemed the obvious choice. I'd always been the tough one, growing up with my three brothers who were skinny, fast, and more athletic than I. I was a little more pleasantly plump, so I knew I wasn't going to find my identity in sports. School was out as well; it seemed no matter how hard I tried, I just couldn't figure it out in the classroom. But despite what I felt I couldn't do, I did believe I was pretty strong for my present age and could tolerate pain well. My dad used to jokingly say, "You're not that smart, so you better get strong." He may have been kidding, but his statement turned into something much more in my mind. It became what I believed.

Hello, false identity.

So, tough it out it was. I found a solid knee brace, with metal brackets on the sides to brace the impact of my steps, and determined to prove I could gut it out and heal myself through good, old fashioned effort. And why not? Ever since I could remember, I was all about trying to make up for what I wasn't by working hard for everything I had—all to earn the right to say I had value as a human being.

When Hannah and I walked the Camino de Santiago that first time in 2015, the main goal was to see Spain and hike those 500 miles, which seemed both daunting and easy at the same time. Thirty days of hiking is a lot, and the mileage is a ton of distance to cover with a bum knee, but I had my new brace, and even with the condition of my knee, my thinking was, "It's only walking. How hard is it to walk? Can't be that hard, right?"

Turned out, it could be pretty rough. Like a big 'ol dummy, I chose not to wear my knee brace as the trek began. The first 12.5 miles wound straight up a mountain, and by the time we hit the summit, I was in serious pain. Why didn't I put on the brace? I thought, and then answered myself with, Oh, that's right. Tough guy. But I kept trekking along as we started down the other side of the mountain. Going down always sucks because it's way easier to slip, and you end up straining your muscles. Most of all, each step slams your joints with a lot more pressure. It's like gravity is sucking your foot down, and when it hits the ground you can feel the crunch inside your knee. I was in so much pain that I couldn't think anymore.

Feeling a little embarrassed and a lot like a sissy, I told Hannah that I had to stop and put on the brace. She was glad I was trying to relieve my pain. However, by then I had waited too long, and the brace didn't help, so I found a branch strong enough to hold my weight and used it as walking stick, sometimes bending the weak knee and using the stick for balance as I hopped down the trail. Needless to say, by the time we got to the first hostel for the night at the Albergue de Peregrinos, I was hobbling around like a 90-year-old stepping on nails. I was desperate for some painkillers and a place to sit and elevate my leg. I found both at the hostel, and I also bought a real walking stick to replace the branch I'd found.

For her part, Hannah was exhausted and sore. Everything hurt, from the blisters on her toes to her aching shoulders and back from carrying her pack. That day we walked just shy of 16 miles, and it seemed we visited three different worlds in the process. We were soaked with sweat from the heat at the start in Saint Jean Pied de Port, then blinded by the fog as we walked up the mountain and sometimes couldn't see ten feet in front of us. We finished the day crunching through the remnant of snow left over from the winter before.

It was so grueling for Hannah that we feared we might have to quit. At one point, on the portion of the route that skirted the France-Spain border, we came across a fruit cart parked on a huge grassy hill where we had a view into France as far as the eye could see. After buying two bananas and some orange juice, Hannah flung off her pack and wearily flopped down on the side of the hill. She looked like she was about to burst into tears. A few minutes later, a Swedish guy decided to sit near us. Hannah asked him how far we had left, and he replied that we had about five kilometers to go.

She looked at me and then at him. "Do you think we'll make it?" she asked, the fatigue evident in her voice.

Cheerfully, he blurted out, "We must!"

For some reason, that made both of us laugh. I think it was from the combination of his excitement, his accent, and our tiredness—but it gave us the will to see the day through.

In all, that first day was wonderful. Sure, we argued a little. I wanted her to go faster, and she wanted me to go slower. But the majority of the time we talked, laughed, and encouraged each other while taking in the scenery. We saw pasturelands, rolling hills, forests, and quaint little towns along the steady mountain incline, and I was experiencing it with the person I loved the most. Despite the pain, how could it be anything else but wonderful?

That first overnight had its whimsical memories, too. We arrived at the monastery too late to get a bed inside the building, but our hosts had anticipated a lot of pilgrims and set up a bunch of small cubed pods outside. The idea of sleeping in one of those freaked me out a bit, because each little pod slept six people with next to no room for movement. We had only about two feet of space inside the entrance before the bunk beds began. The monastery also had a larger mobile restroom with showers for the latecomers. Hannah and I selected a pod, dropped our packs in the bunks, and headed for the showers.

"I hope the showers are enclosed," I commented to Hannah as we approached the restroom. "The last thing I want to see is a bunch of old, naked dudes."

Sometimes you just don't get what you want in life. The stalls indeed were enclosed, but I still saw an old, fat Canadian fall out of one, yelling obscenities as he plummeted to the floor. He grabbed the shower curtain on his way down, but he somehow managed to land on his back on top of the curtain, leaving him uncovered. Instead of grabbing for a towel or his clothes, he just laid there spread eagle, revealing all his glory. To make it even more awkward, he just stared at me, and I did everything I could to maintain eye contact so I wouldn't catch a glimpse of "little Canada." After a few seconds during which we both realized how weird it was, I helped the old guy to his feet. We spoke for a moment, and then he got into a different shower. I know we are in Europe, I thought, but this is ridiculous.

Still, it wasn't as embarrassing as the next morning when, after a night of deep sleep, I woke up in the tiny pod with my head turned directly toward the nude butt cheeks of two college girls. One of their headlamps was turned on, providing just enough light to know exactly what I was seeing. They were getting dressed, but all they had on at that moment were their bras and thongs. You've gotta be kidding me, I thought, and immediately turned my head away, only to see my wife looking over at me from her nearby bunk. She thinks I was checking out their butts. This is not a good way to start the day.

And it was only going to get better as the day wore on.

Hannah and I laughed off the unintended peep show as we skipped breakfast and hit the trail before the sun rose. We weren't hungry and wanted to get an early start. As the sun crested above the horizon, we were on a little path just outside of Roncesvalles, the village in northern Spain where the first albergue was located. There is something to be said about the slow illumination of the world around you. In those moments is a quiet beauty, and we took it in together, reveling in its peaceful simplicity.

Whenever we go on long hikes or journeys like the Camino de Santiago, Hannah and I are polar opposites. I could spend the entire time not saying a word to another soul and love every moment. I embrace the solitude and aloneness of it all. However, that would destroy Hannah. She thrives on meeting people and forming new relationships. It's not that I don't like people, but more that I don't like meeting new people. It's uncomfortable for me. I don't really know what to do or what to say. My wife says I make a terrible first impression. Hannah, on the other hand, loves everyone from the moment she sees them. She has an innate ability to genuinely care for others and their lives. From the moment you meet Hannah, you feel like she's your best friend.

So, it's no wonder, that on the first day alone, she made a few new friends, chatting it up with them as they walked together. Usually, the conversation started with, "Where are you from?" and "Why are you walking the Camino?" and then I'd introduce myself and listen the rest of the time. Since Hannah moves faster when she's engrossed in conversation, I was all for it because I wanted us to keep going. One girl we met within the first 100 yards of the trek walked with us for the remainder of the Camino. Within that same day, we took a break to sit on a wall next to a lady who had to be in her late sixties. I wanted to keep walking, but Hannah insisted we meet her and hear all about why she was there. I don't remember what she said, but I guarantee you Hannah could recall and relay her entire story.

As the morning progressed on day two, the weather quickly warmed so that by late morning it was hot enough to make us both miserable. We stopped for a bite to eat around 10:00 a.m. at a little hole in the wall place with plastic tables and chairs outside. We both ordered "tortilla," which in Spain is something like a potato breakfast pie, and I ordered an Americano because drip coffee is not available there. Hannah and I ate, rested, nursed our calves and quads, and I took off my knee brace to let my leg breathe a bit.

After a half-hour, we were back on the trail again. I didn't want to waste too much time because that could mean we wouldn't get a bed at the next albergue. Hannah didn't seem too concerned about that, which frustrated me and caused us to bicker. Instead of enjoying the scenery as I had the day before, I began to keep to myself, silently running our pace through my mind and estimating how fast we had to walk to arrive early enough to claim a bed in the next town, Larrasoaña. I got caught up in my own fear of not making it in time. I looked from the path, to my watch, and back down to the path, oblivious of everything else, including Hannah and whomever she happened to be talking to. I was stressing myself out instead of taking in the history and experiencing the freedom of the outdoors as I had planned.

Around one in the afternoon, we were walking near a large stream that separated the trail from a town called Zubiri, which had a main cobble street with a few homes and shops on each side. The path led to a fork. One path continued the Camino route; the other led down a little dusty slope headed toward the town. A few pilgrims had gone that direction, which featured a small stone bridge spanning a lovely, clear water stream. Several people sat on the bank of the stream soaking their feet in the cool water. They were visiting and relaxing—which, at that moment, seemed to stress me out even more. I don't know why. The town seemed like a nice place to rest, and what did it really matter to me what they were doing anyway? Besides, Hannah and I were both exhausted despite the earlier food break.

Hannah looked at me. "We should go down and take a break," she said.

I could tell that she was asking—no, deep down, begging—to take a break. I could see the longing in her eyes and the excitement in her face at the prospect of chatting with the other pilgrims.

I thought about it for a second, but my mind was already made up. I looked at my watch and calculated how far we still had to go. If we didn't get a bed, we were going to have to walk all the way to the next town, getting in later and having a more difficult time finding a place to stay.

"I don't think we should stop," I said, leaning on my walking stick. "We've gotta keep going."

Hannah gently pressed. "But wouldn't it be nice to rest, just for a little bit, and put our feet in the water?"

I did want to put my feet in, but that meant taking off our boots and socks, then needing to wait for our feet to dry before we could put them back on. Hiking with wet feet is a terrible idea. This wasn't going to be a five-minute break. It was going to be a delay of at least 20 minutes, maybe longer. That's plenty of time for other pilgrims to snag our beds.

"We really need to keep going," I insisted. "We've already stopped two minutes." Yes, I was actually timing it.

She relented with a sigh and I saw her shoulders, burdened with her pack, slump a little. We trekked on. The way I looked at it, I was doing her a favor. She'd certainly thank me for it later.

But that wasn't the truth. No, not at all.

I didn't realize it then, or even for the rest of the Camino, but I wasn't doing her a favor at all. My fear of not making it to the next town in time to get a bed was greater than our need to rest, and worse still, greater than my desire to let my wife have a rest or let her put her feet in the stream. She really wanted to, but I wouldn't let her. Later that day, she sat under a tree and cried because her feet hurt so much. She cried every day about 10 miles into that day's walk, but this cry was far worse. It was as if she was mourning.

It took me the entire trip, the flight back to the States, and then a few days more before I realized that in that moment, selfish fear overcame unconditional love. I did not love my wife well. Even today, when I think back to that stop by the stream, I feel sick. I feel shame. I apologized, and though Hannah has forgiven me—even though God has forgiven me—it remains a stain on my memory.

Recalling that day makes me consider deeply what it means to love others as myself. According to Jesus, the two greatest commands are to love God and to love those around us. I know what He said. I believe it, but do I really understand it? Has it changed the way I live? How can I say I love others when I struggle to love my own wife the way I'm supposed to? How do I get to the place where fear doesn't overcome love, and we can put our feet in the stream? I don't know exactly what it looks like, but I determined if I ever got to walk the Camino again, I was going to do my best to find out. Next time, my focus was going to be meditating on the question, "What does it really mean to love God and to love others?" It might be spurred on by regret, but it was not going to be a journey of atonement. It was going to be one of discovery and growth.

Hannah sat under that tree and wept for about ten minutes while I waffled between trying to encourage her and hiding my frustration that we weren't making any progress. Eventually, I helped her up and we continued on the path toward Larrasoaña. I continued, too, with my tiresome ritual of stressing, checking my watch, and calculating our speed. The constant struggle of slowing myself down so Hannah could keep up made the walk far more difficult than it should have been. I could feel the urgency of covering distance clashing with the knowledge that she needed a slower pace. It was much like driving a car with a manual transmission for the first time. You press the gas and let the clutch out, waiting to feel the moment the gears lock, but instead all you get is a hard jerk forward and then a stall. The whole rest of the day felt like that. I'd lurch forward, realize Hannah was no longer in sight, and then stop and wait. She'd catch up, and I'd hit the gas, only to soon find another place to halt.

Jerk. Stall. Repeat.

My frustration steadily grew, but I knew I had to keep it under wraps after the weeping tree episode. Every now and then I tried to look patient and offered a semi-hearty, "You got this, babe," with an encouraging smile and false cheerfulness. At the same time, I was realizing that my self-imposed anxiety was taking an ever-increasing toll on my body as well as my psyche. I felt heavier and walked with a slouch as though I was dragging a tree stump behind me, despite the fact that the trail was actually easier underfoot. Most of it was covered with trees, so the sun didn't pound on us as it had the morning before.

You need to chill out, chided a stern voice in my head. It was a good idea, and I did try, but at every attempt, failure ensued. I could not relax. I had to make sure that Hannah and I snagged a proper place to sleep that night. No more bunks in the tiny pod. No more naked guys at night and naked butts in the morning.

But it wasn't all bad for the two of us. Sure, we frustrated each other along the way, but it seemed we made it over the hump after the tree incident, and we had no more disastrous weeping sessions. We even started empathizing with each other, with Hannah giving me permission to pace ahead of her as long as I didn't get too far away. It didn't really change the circumstances, but it did make me feel like I had a little more freedom. We also agreed that instead of having big breakdown moments, it would be better for Hannah to walk and cry at the same time. Since part of what makes the Camino difficult is that sense that you're never going to get to the end of that day's journey, it might be better if she could express her emotion while making progress toward her goal. That became a mantra for Hannah: "Walk and cry, walk and cry."

In the end, we walked into Larrasoaña later than I wanted—but way earlier than a lot of others who had spent the day lollygagging. This town also had more than one place to stay, so when we learned that the primary albergue was full, we found a nice little hostel that cost us an extra few Euros but had fewer people to a room. After checking in, we walked up a narrow stairway to a room that had four beds divided by a few feet of walkway between each one. The blankets reminded me of those my grandmother would have used in her guest bedroom. It was comfortable but, quite frankly, I would've settled for burlap blankets, because all I wanted was to take off my pack and boots.

We dropped our gear and lay down for a few minutes. Hannah closed her eyes while I examined the new blisters that had popped up on my right pinky toe. I should probably name this one, I thought as I poked at the biggest bubble with my finger. "Jumbo" would've been appropriate, because it later became large enough to engulf the entire toe and make me look like I had leprosy.

Hannah and I were hungry, so before long we peeled off our sweaty clothes, exchanged our boots for sandals, and trudged out in search of a restaurant. The town wasn't anything amazing, but it held a quaint beauty and seemed to whisper that it had a significant amount of history. Unfortunately, I was too tired and famished to explore that.

It took us a few minutes, but we finally found the eatery, which felt more like a bar than a restaurant. Thick wooden beams, spaced a few feet apart from one another, sectioned off the white ceiling, which was a stark contrast to the tan Spanish tile on the floor. Long picnic tables were crammed in next to one another to accommodate all the travelers, making the space feel as cramped as it was. It was packed with pilgrims and the roar of voices was almost overbearing as we stepped inside.

We plopped down at a table with eight others and ordered some food from plastic-covered menus that had pictures next to almost every dish so that non-Spanish speakers like Hannah and me could figure out what the deuce we were ordering. The wine was cheap. We'd heard a couple of Euros could get us a really good bottle anywhere throughout Spain, but I'm not a big fan of the grape. Try as they might, no one has convinced me there's a wine that tastes as good as whiskey. But I was obviously the only one in the place with this aversion because it seemed Hannah and I were the only ones present who hadn't already consumed a glass or two.

It was also apparent that tipsy pilgrims were louder and loved to talk about the different bumps or bruises they had sustained that day. Eventually the conversation at our table moved to the subject of what everyone thought was the most difficult part of the Camino so far.

Hannah immersed herself in the stories and opinions. I mostly wondered how long it would take for dinner to arrive.

One of the people at our table, a red-haired Irish girl in her early twenties, boasted about how she wasn't having any problems at all. She wasn't even sore. "I thought it would be harder," she heralded even louder than she had been speaking before. I found myself getting annoyed with her. I have little tolerance for braggarts.

She then looked at me and asked, "What do you think?"

I thought for a moment. "I'm definitely sore," I said, "but I think it would be way easier if I could walk at my own pace. I keep having to slow down so I don't lose Hannah, and it's making me strain myself more than I should."

As the words left my mouth, I realized that I sounded like a huge jerk, making it seem that somehow Hannah was causing my problems when that was not what I meant at all. A verse in the book of Proverbs says, "I am more stupid than any man." I used to think it was funny. Now I realize it's about me.

Thankfully, Hannah didn't wince at my statement. I think she actually understood that I was simply telling the truth. Either that, or she had become really good at hiding frustration with her husband. She's always had supreme patience with me and my stupidity.

But someone else had a big problem with what I said.

"I call bullshit!" It was the red-haired girl, whose delightful retort was blurted loud enough to get the attention of everyone at our table.

Caught utterly off guard, I stayed silent for a second while eight sets of eyes stared at me.

"Well, it's the truth," I spoke as calmly as I could. My ears got hot and I knew my face was turning red, not from embarrassment, but anger. Who was she to say what I find difficult and to call me out like that? What an arrogant little turd. The fact that she was getting drunk didn't hinder my harsh inner dialogue. I struggle to love people when it's not convenient.

I didn't say anything else. She moved on to the next person, and I gladly let her.

The food was finally served, and I scarfed it down like it was the last meal I'd ever eat. I consoled my indignation by thinking that the Irish girl would probably quit before she finished the journey. A lot of people brag to cover their weakness.

In all, Hannah and I were at the restaurant for about an hour and a half before heading back to the hostel and into our beds for the night.

After all, we needed to get up early the next morning to do it all over again—and I had no way of knowing what was going to come next.

THE NEXT DAY'S WALK FROM LARRASOAÑA TO PAMPLONA WAS THE shortest of the entire Camino. It was only about 10 miles, and since we left around six in the morning, we walked into town before the albergue was even open to accept new pilgrims.

The day was beautiful, not too hot or too chilly, and when I saw that the journey was going to be brief, I wasn't worried about getting into town too late to get a bed. Early on, we didn't see a soul, probably because everyone was still sleeping off their wine and stories from the night before. Hannah and I walked through a few towns that resembled one another yet at the same time were nothing like we had ever seen back home. Cobblestone streets were surrounded by aged buildings held together with a mixture of old stones and newer plaster. We crossed over rolling hills that slowly descended toward Pamplona. Worn stone huts housing sheep and other livestock were scattered along hills with rocks covered in thick dew-laden moss, and views that stretched on for miles.

I was actually enjoying myself.

Shots of pain from my left knee interrupted the pleasantness every once in a while, but I found the heavier I leaned into my staff, the less pain I felt. I called it a "staff" rather than a walking stick because it sounded manlier. I conjured up images of Moses lifting his staff to part the Red Sea or smiting the rock in anger so that water erupted from it. He led millions of people across a desert to the Promised Land while leaning on a staff. A walking stick is something old people use when carrying day packs filled with snacks that my little daughter could haul around while walking in her plastic sandals. Yes, staff is better than walking stick, even if I am overcompensating when I use the word.

Atop a grass-covered hill a few hours outside Pamplona, we met a Canadian in his forties. I was a little reluctant as he cheerfully greeted us, "Buen Camino!" It literally translates "good road" in Spanish and was the official greeting among pilgrims on the journey. By then, I'd heard it hundreds of times to the point of utter annoyance. The man, not fat but certainly a little more than pudgy, became a friend we met up with every few days, mostly because he was a people-person like Hannah. Being the kind-hearted person that I am, I immediately thought, "This guy probably won't make it." I later found out he had the same thought about us as he watched me limp my way along the trail.

For some reason, after listening to him and Hannah chat for a mile or so, I found myself wanting to engage in conversation with the two of them. As we trekked, I reasoned, Today is different. It's more cheerful, more freeing than the past two days. Maybe a new leaf has turned.

We left him behind at a café in a town so small its name slips my memory. Hannah and I pushed on, not because I was forcing her, but to simply keep walking and talking with each other. She always asks really good questions that lead to deep discussions of spirituality, love, and what we believe about ourselves. Hannah can dig anything out of me effortlessly, mostly because I can't help but want to tell her everything about myself and discover everything there is to know about her.

We entered Pamplona just before 11:00 in the morning and found the albergue without a problem. Since it wasn't open, we took off our packs and leaned them against the wall next to the door. There we waited, with Hannah content to do so because she wanted to sit down. I was more concerned about making sure we didn't lose our spot in line, which was a miniscule possibility because we had arrived so early.

As I counted the others beginning to gather around, I heard a familiar squeal. It's the noise Hannah makes when she sees someone she loves but hasn't been with in a while. I quickly turned my head to see the girl she made friends with back on Day One. She was standing next to a guy in shorts that were short enough to remind me of pictures I had seen of my dad from the 1970s. I remained quiet while Hannah and the girl hugged and started talking about—well, who knows? I just remember shorts guy. The two of us stared at one each other awkwardly as I tried to figure out which one of us was going to introduce himself first since the girls were already lost in telling stories.

I took the lead. "Hi, I'm Nick," and I stretched out my right arm to shake his hand.

He had a strong grip and gave his name, at which point our conversation ceased. We both decided it was better to listen to the squeaky excitement of the girls rather than continue with our exchange—which worked out perfectly because that was the moment the doors to the albergue opened up to take us all in.

We shouldered our packs and walked inside to a small foyer with a desk in the middle of the room. Behind it was a Spanish lady in her mid-fifties ready to check us in.

"Passport," she said to each one of us as we walked up to her. She wanted to see our pilgrim's passports, which were essential to stay at the albergues and to receive certificates of completion once we arrived in Santiago. The trifolded paper was stamped at each place to prove we walked the route. Each albergue had an officially certified stamp that could be verified to ensure no one faked the pilgrimage, although I couldn't imagine why anyone would want to do so.

After our passports were stamped, we walked into a huge room with white tiled floors that reflected the fluorescent lights on the ceiling. It smelled like the floors had just been bleached, and the identical bunk beds lined in rows were perfectly made with white pillowcases resting on top of green blankets. The whole place seemed a little too clean, making it more like a hospital than an albergue.

The four of us -- Short Shorts, myself, Hannah, and her new best friend -- found bunks next to one another and dropped our packs on the floor, in obedience to the signs posted everywhere with a picture of a pack on a bed crossed out. Hannah lay down on the bed with a sigh of relief and we all made plans to explore Pamplona, but not before a quick shower. Since we were some of the first pilgrims to make it in, we knew we could have hot water now that may not be available later in the day as more people arrived.

After we all showered and changed, we donned our sandals and walked toward the main square of town, the plaza mayor. The soles of my feet were freakishly tender from the previous days, and even though I was wearing sandals, it felt like I was walking barefoot and stepping on Legos. I kept wrenching my body around trying to make it hurt less while also trying to hide the pain. I should've had my staff with me to help alleviate the discomfort, but for some reason I thought it would be weird to walk around the city clutching a big stick, so I left it behind. Short Shorts and Best Friend were walking briskly and didn't seem to hurt at all. I knew Hannah was sore like me, but because she was in conversation, she kept up the pace with no problem.

When we finally made it to the plaza (by "finally" I mean that it only took a few minutes, but my feet made it feel like an hour had passed), we found a non-descript white plastic table with matching white chairs outside of a restaurant. I don't recall its name, mostly because we chose it for the view it gave of the entire square. We decided to sit down and have a drink. I had gin with Short Shorts while the girls relaxed with wine.

What we had intended to be a few minutes turned into hours as we ate tapas, talked, and people-watched. I learned Short Shorts had just gotten out of the U.S. Army. He told us the Camino was the first decision he made on his own since being sent to military school as a kid. When someone brought up the obscenely short shorts he was wearing, he smirked and said they were called "Ranger Panties." The three of us erupted in laughter, and I choked a little on my drink. This guy had made it through West Point and then served overseas and somehow ended up wearing panties.

Not so funny, though, was when I noticed Hannah becoming a little less talkative and her face looking pale.

"I don't feel very good," she said, the words coming out weak. "I think I might puke."

I looked at her wine glass. She hadn't even finished it, so I knew she hadn't had enough of it to get sick. Then I remembered the times she had gotten sick on past trips: on our first day in Nepal she ended up laying down for hours to recover; on our third day in Puerto Villarta I spent most of the night holding back her hair as she yacked into the porcelain god; and on our honeymoon in Honduras she got sick after we had stopped to eat.

It must be the food, I thought. When Hannah travels, she always gets sick at some point from food she's not used to eating. Short Shorts and Best Friend helped me guide her back to the albergue and onto her bunk. As they asked her questions trying to figure out what was wrong, I suggested it was the tapas. But as Hannah lay down, Best Friend queried, "How much water have you had today?"

None. Her answer was none.

How in the world do you walk ten miles and then drink and eat for a few hours without ever drinking water? Instantly I was worried and angry at the same time. I tried to be helpful and caring while also commenting a little too aggressively about the importance of staying hydrated when hiking. Best Friend didn't seem to be bothered by it at all. In fact, she was prepared, offering Hannah a bottle of water with an electrolyte tab dissolving in it. "Just drink this," she told Hannah, "and you'll feel better in a bit."

Hannah gratefully took the bottle and began sipping on it, and I covered her up with the green blanket. Our friends then decided they wanted to go back out to explore Pamplona and invited me to come along. There was still time because it was only four o'clock, but there was no way I was going to leave Hannah. Not only would that make me a bad husband, but my feet still felt like someone had hit them with a meat tenderizer.

The albergue that seemed like a hospital had suddenly become one for Hannah, making me grateful for the uber-cleanliness I'd criticized earlier. After Short Shorts and Best Friend departed, I climbed into the bunk above Hannah and started to read. I had brought five books with me—everything from biographies to theology to business—intending to read them on the trip. I cracked open the one about how to successfully build businesses, intermittently checking in on Hannah to see if she was feeling better. Each time, she seemed a little better and spoke slightly softer. Her body was rehydrating, but she was exhausted.

The forced break was good for me. For once, I wasn't worried about tomorrow or what time we were going to make it to the next albergue, and as Hannah recovered, I found myself enjoying the simple pleasure of reading my book. Before long, I concluded that turning in early was a great idea. I checked in on Hannah one last time, found her sound asleep, and noticed it was eight o'clock. I decided to roll over and get some shut eye. I was out in no time.

It was the calm before the emotional storm that was about to blow in.

I woke up the next morning before my alarm went off. Annoyed at the premature intrusion into my slumber, I rolled to one side to get comfortable, then to the other, and back again. There's no way I'm falling back asleep, I thought to myself, feeling like I was being robbed of the wonderful sleep I could be getting. I quietly peaked my head over the edge of the bed to see if Hannah was still asleep. She was just beginning to stir, and I figured she'd be opening her eyes in about five minutes. I lay back on my stomach with my arm drooped over the edge waiting for her to wake up.

Seven minutes later she still wasn't awake, but I had to go to the bathroom. I slipped out of my sleeping bag and, with my foot, felt for the first step on the ladder to get down. I found it, but the second step wasn't where I thought it was going to be. My exposed shin scraped the rung, and I grunted as quietly as I could while pain shocked me fully awake.

Still dangling over the end, I carefully stepped down onto Hannah's bed as a slew of Christian curse words ran through my mind. Christian cursing is the phenomenon where believers use "frick," "sweet Jemima," "dagnabbit," and a plethora of other phrases to express the exact same feeling a good ol' unholy phrase would capture. Apparently, God can't tell what we actually mean if we substitute an "r-i" for a "u" in a moment of distress. It must be a loophole in the doctrine of omniscience.

Of course, the commotion woke Hannah and I apologized as I reached the floor and rubbed my shin, checking to see if I was bleeding. It was just a scratch.

"Is it time to get up?" she asked in a hushed tone.

"Not yet, but I have to pee," I responded. The urgency in my bladder apparently made the announcement come out of my mouth louder than I desired.

When I returned, Hannah was already sitting up and packing her things into her bag, using a tiny pink flashlight to see what she was doing. I leaned down next to her ear to whisper. "You wanna hit the road?" I asked.

"Yeah," she replied softly. "I'm not tired."

We were out before the sun was up but making our way out of Pamplona while it was still dark was a little more difficult than anticipated. I missed one of the Camino signs, an easy-to-see yellow arrow or an outline of a seashell in bright yellow with a blue backdrop, but we eventually found the path again and began our walk out of the city.

Hannah and I agreed to cover ten miles by ten o'clock so that we could avoid walking during the heat of the day. From then on, "ten by ten" became our daily morning ritual. When the time came to stop, we entered a little town that hardly lived up to that description. There was one street that couldn't have been longer than a mile with buildings lining each side. It looked like a giant had taken a town and smashed all the buildings together so that they were perfectly straight, each building sharing the wall of the adjacent structure. I stopped and cupped my hands against the glass to look inside each one.

"Babe!" Hannah half whispered, half shouted. "What if someone is in there?"

Sometimes my curiosity trumps common sense and I end up

looking like a creeper. I shrugged. "They're all closed or empty."

She grimaced and frowned as I decided to walk in the middle of the street with her and pretend that I wasn't still trying to peer past our reflections and into the windows.

We eventually found a few businesses open including a little café, and I walked in, ordered tortillas, and snagged an Americano for myself. Hannah stayed outside and sat down at a table. When I walked out and saw her sipping from her water bottle, the fear and frustration of the night before popped into my mind. I considered making a snarky comment but realized that was a bad idea. I was just relieved to see her drinking water. I sat down next to her without saying a word.

"I'm drinking my water," she immediately said, her tone slightly accusatory.

She knew what I was thinking. I have no clue how she does that, but when she does it, she's almost always right.

"That's good," I said, striving to sound sweet rather than negative. "I don't want you to get sick again." Hannah smiled, and I am pretty sure she knew that I was holding back something more sarcastic. I slurped my coffee to avoid burning my tongue and noticed how she was looking at me, her smile slowly getting bigger. My wife's smile is something else. It always makes me smile, too. We sat and stared at each other, grins on our faces, waiting for our tortillas. It's in those moments that I am reminded all over again how much I love her.

Sitting outside as the morning chill wore off, we talked about the day before and the walk to come. A truck pulled up close to us, and we watched as a few people came out of the store next to the café and started loading it with boxes. A few minutes later, we heard a familiar voice and saw Short Shorts walking toward us with Best Friend next to him. How in the world did they catch up to us so fast, I thought. Hannah was elated to see them, and the four of us sat around the table for fifteen minutes as we finished our food before heading off together toward Puente la Reina.

We each had our own pace due to a combination of leg length and motivation. Best Friend was tall and thin and strode with the freedom and confidence of someone out to explore the world. Short Shorts didn't really walk. It was more of a mini-jog as he kept up with Best Friend, obviously driven to stay with her. Hannah, at five-foot-three-inches, has short little legs which made her take almost double the amount of steps as the rest of us. I treaded somewhere in the middle of our group. Keeping up wasn't difficult, but it was not necessarily comfortable either, with me hobbling along on my staff. My bum knee apparently gave me a slight limp and a tendency to drift off to the left as I walked. I was no Quasimodo, but I definitely had a hitch in my giddy-up.

All of this was quickly evident as Short Shorts and Best Friend had to continually slow down to avoid getting ahead of us. Before long, she announced, "We're gonna go on ahead," and they quickly left us in the dust.

Hannah and I fell into a steady pace, and I found myself much more relaxed from the night before. The urgency of making sure we made it to the next place faded, and my eyes began to roam the landscape, taking in the rolling hills and wheat fields. The birds in the nearby trees whistled and chirped to one another, providing a cheery, lighthearted soundtrack for the walk. I grinned and noticed that I was going faster. My limp decreased, too, to the point I started twirling my staff instead of leaning on it. Before long, Hannah was well behind me.

Man, look where you are! I thought. You're freaking walking across Spain and you don't have to do anything else. No responsibility. No work. Just hiking with your wife and God. I was truly experiencing His creation for the first time since the Camino started. I even began praying quietly.

I was totally free.

Then something happened to me—or, more accurately, in me. I suddenly stopped, and as I gazed across a huge field with tall golden wheat bending slightly in the wind, I realized I was scared. Really scared. It was as if I had just been pushed out of a plane without a chute. Raw fear rushed across my face and filled my lungs. My chest hurt. My muscles tensed. I grasped my staff so hard my knuckles turned white.

I don't know what to do. I thought. I've never walked with God.

I was 18 and at Bible college when I became a follower of Jesus. A mere nine months later, I took a full-time position at a church in Ramona, California, as a youth pastor. I shouldn't have been offered the job, much less taken it. I had no clue what to do, and no idea of what following Jesus was really all about. Immature and unprepared, I put my nose to the grindstone and went to work for God, trying to finish school and minister to teenagers at the same time. I half-heartedly completed getting my degree in theology because I devoted most of my time and energy to my duties for the church.

I kept that up for five years before deciding that God was calling me to be a college pastor at a church in Tucson. The students and leaders hated the direction I was starting to take the group, and I was promptly fired. But, surprisingly, I was offered free use of the youth room to launch my own church as a senior pastor.

I did exactly that—but since I wasn't earning a salary with the new church, I took on employment as a mail carrier. The only problem was the contract had me working Monday through Saturday, leaving me evenings and Sundays to take care of the church. So, I worked for God and delivered mail. I didn't take a day off for two years before finally finding another contractor to take a few days a week on the mail route so I could focus more on trying to be a pastor.

When people told me, "Man, you work a lot," I took it as a huge compliment.

Look how hard I work for God.

That's what separates me from the norm.

That's what makes me a good Christian.

Six years later, my church was established, and I had even allowed myself time for a few vacations. But I created a pattern in my life of working so hard that my body would shut down and force me to lie in bed until I recuperated. After a few days, I'd get up and start doing it all over again.

That was when Hannah suggested going on the Camino, and my board of elders strongly agreed I needed to take a longer break because they said I worked too much.

Now here I was, frozen in the middle of a walking trail in Spain, racked with fear because I only knew how to work for God, not walk with Him.

How do I walk with God? My mind raced. How can I when God wants me to work. That's the only reason I'm around, isn't it? To work for Him? He didn't want to go on this walk with me. I don't know if He even loves me.

Tears filled my eyes. My stomach dropped.

Then a second revelation hit me. It wasn't that God didn't love me. That's dumb. Actually, I was using work as a means of forcing God to love me. Surely, He had to accept me after all the hours, all the late nights, and all the effort I'd put in for Him. I instantly felt like a child again, back when I had nothing else to offer anyone but to work hard. It was the only way I was validated and praised by the adults in my life. It was how I controlled them, and how I gave myself value. So, it was easy to simply transpose that onto God.

I work for you, Lord, and you have to love me.

That realization made me feel gross. Low. As dirty as a worm wriggling around in the dirt—the dirt God made—demanding that He submit.

That's when a final certainty struck home. God didn't love me because I was trying to control Him. I had never given God the opportunity to love me because of my control.

With that, a wave of truth washed through me like a warm breeze, and God spoke to my newly awakened spirit. He said, "I want to walk with you. I want you to know I love you regardless of how hard you work or the ways you try to control me."

I closed my eyes as tightly as I could, trying not to lose the moment: a punch to my soul followed by a tender but strong hug from the Holy Spirit. The intense fear vanished. The chute opened, and I was floating downward, cradled safely in His arms.

I looked out over the flaxen field, heard the birds chirping their merry songs, and I was totally free once again—even more than before. Now, I was free from having to force God to love me. Free to be loved without reserve.

I was free to walk the Camino with Him.

I began shouting, laughing uncontrollably, and whirling and twirling my staff while throwing it into the air. People were coming toward me on the path, and I must have looked insane. Maybe I was, but I kept up my antics, causing many to stare at me as they passed. Aware of the scene I was making, I tried to subdue myself by holding my staff steady, but I still couldn't stop laughing. The joy gushed from within me. The strangers picked up their pace while avoiding eye contact. I just gave them a great story. Remember the crazy laughing guy leaning on a stick in the middle of nowhere. Yeah, that's what they're gonna say.

Hannah had fallen behind farther than I thought, so it took her longer than I expected to catch up to me. By the time I finally spied her meandering toward me, I had managed to fully compose myself, but I still had a huge smile on my face.

"You look happy, babe," she said, her eyes sparkling with obvious excitement at my mood.

"I am!" My voice was louder and more jubilant than I expected.

"Why are you so happy?" Her face gleamed. She was clearly delighted because she saw I was.

I opened my mouth to speak, to share the insanity that had just happened, to reveal the life-altering moment I just had with God—but all that came out was a long, deep, audible breath. Some things take longer than others to put into words, and this was definitely one of them.

"I just love the outdoors," I said, wishing that I could make her feel what I was experiencing. "It's where I feel the closest to God."

"I love that about you," she replied genuinely as we turned to continue down the trail.

Once more, I was reminded how Hannah is the love of my life. There was no one else I wanted by my side after such a huge spiritual awakening. When I was finally able to put words to my experience a few days later, Hannah listened intently, and then once again gave me that "something else" smile of hers as she caught a glimpse of what had happened in my heart and spirit.

As for the rest of that day, I don't remember anything else. The scenery, monasteries, and conversations leading into Puente la Reina were eclipsed by the moment God met me and peeled back a few layers of my heart. That moment, in fact, overshadowed the rest of my experiences on the Camino de Santiago and became the pinnacle of the journey. That's not meant to downplay the rest of the pilgrimage. I look back at it with wonderful memories—ones that make my heart yearn to return.

Over the remaining 25 days, Hannah and I trekked through places like Burgos, where we marveled at the architecture and rich history of the town that once had a resident "warlord." We visited León, which rests next to a river and got its name from a Roman military garrison. The seventh legion made the city its base and named it after the word meaning "legion." Astorga was memorable, too, for its Old Town, a huge market with shops and historic buildings tightly packed within medieval walls.

Along the way, Hannah and I each placed a rock at the foot of the Cruz de Ferro, an iron cross erected atop a five-meter wooden pole where, tradition holds, one symbolically leaves his burdens behind at the feet of Christ. At Monasterio de Irache, a former Benedictine monastery attached to a winery, pilgrims were encouraged to sample the free vino flowing from the "wine fountain." The castle of the Knights Templar captured our imaginations as we walked the walls and courtyards steeped in lore. Everywhere we went, depictions of the Virgin Mary and Christ on the cross became daily sights as we sat in old cathedral pews or wandered around to touch ancient stone walls.

Near the end of the Camino, on the way to O'Cebreiro, Hannah heard about a place where we could rent horses to ride up the mountain into the village. I refused the equestrian aid, determined to walk the entire path, but Hannah rode while I jogged beside her and her horse. Just shy of O'Cebreiro we caught up with Short Shorts and Best Friend, who asked why I chose to run up the mountain alongside my wife and her steed. "I don't know. I just did," I replied. It was instinctual to simply want to be with her instead of falling behind and catching up to her later.

Short Shorts and Best Friend remained steady companions, and they became the core of what we started calling our "Camino Family." We laughed and ate. We drank and talked of deep things. We walked and we hurt—and we grew closer. That's what you do when you do difficult things together. We still keep in contact, messaging one another about new trips and big life events, or simply about how much we miss the Camino and one another.

I met two other Christians during the Camino. One was a Hungarian who walked with me for six hours as I blabbed on and on about the Holy Spirit, but she seemed genuinely interested. I could tell she believed in God and personally experienced something with Him while in Spain. I still think of her every once in a while and pray that she thrives in her journey with Jesus. The second was a joyfully plump pastor who was gun-shy about telling other pilgrims about his role in the church. The only reason he told me was because I shared with him about my church in Tucson. I couldn't blame him for not letting others know. People tend to treat you differently when they find out you're a minister. The first thing they usually do is apologize for their language, like our ears are too holy to hear them spout off a few four-letter words. He was probably the happiest person we met on the entire trip. For him, he was a kid again, completely free to laugh and play. We finished the Camino a day ahead of him and gave him a huge hug as he finished his journey.

Then there was a Canadian who walked with us for an entire day on the way into Los Arcos. When he found out I was a pastor, there was no end to his questions. "Why do you believe what you do?" "How do you apply it practically?" "What difference does your faith make in politics or economics?" I was able to share what the Bible said. He didn't become a follower of Jesus, but that doesn't mean he won't.

The climax, of course, was ending the long, sometimes arduous, 500-mile walk at the Cathedral of Santiago. Signs everywhere proclaim, "Santiago is not the end," and perhaps that's true of the significance of the experience, but the Pilgrims Service does formally close the annual event. Several priests oversee the tradition of swinging the "botafumeiro," a large, ornate brass bucket filled with burning embers, which is attached to a rope thrown over a rafter in the cathedral. As has been done since the twelfth century, the cathedral is filled with smoke as the silver chalice swings back and forth at over 40 miles per hour, it's 213-foot arched trajectory covering the massive space. In just 90 seconds, the pilgrims packing the nave are blanketed in the fumes, its scent reminiscent of incense.

For many, the swinging of the "botafumeiro" is the marker that their pilgrimage—their penance or spiritual indulgence—is finished. It is meant to be the physical and symbolic evidence that somehow encapsulates all that they have experienced and worked through during the Camino. The fact that the chalice's true purpose is not spiritual at all, but is actually intended to cover the stench of the pilgrims and to kill any lice attached to them, is secondary or outright ignored in favor of the symbolism of the moment.

That evening, we gathered all of our "Camino Family" into a house we rented for the night and shared a huge steak dinner. We talked and reminisced, wondered about what the future may hold, and made plans to visit one another. I sipped whiskey as I gave my Bible away to someone who said he was now considering spiritual things as a result of the Camino experience. As we congratulated one another on the pilgrimage we made, our gestures were marked with a tinge of sadness. The Camino was over and our party heralded the beginning of our journeys home.

In the end, I did get to experience Christian tradition and enjoy the outdoors. I also had a personal yet significant spiritual experience, even if it had nothing to do with Saint James or his old bones. I walked with God for the first time in my life, and I began to deal with the lies I had chosen to believe about myself. Lies that had defined a life of overworking to earn my sense of value so that I could control God and force Him to love me.

And, walking staff and all, I had met my goal of completing the

Camino.

Question was, would I ever do it again?

"WHERE DID YOU START THE CAMINO?"

It's a common question, one of the first ones asked when two pilgrims meet on the trail. The vast majority of pilgrims commence the journey in France at Saint Jean Pied de Port. Others begin in Spain, in Pamplona or Sarria, and some even start in Paris. After all, there is a difference between where someone begins the pilgrimage versus where one actually starts walking it.

My second pilgrimage actually started 9,000 miles away from Saint Jean Pied de Port, back home in Tucson, with an idea. It was about a year after I finished the first one, and I began to conjure up dreams of opening my own albergue and taking care of pilgrims. Since I met so few Christians the first time, I thought it could be a killer way to kick-start spiritual conversations with the people walking a traditionally Catholic pilgrimage. The plan grew when I mentioned it to James, a friend of mine who grew up as a missionary kid in Africa and was completing a residency program to be a doctor. He was always down for a crazy adventure and a new way to do mission work, and he jumped with both feet into the albergue project. He speculated how we could offer medical care for pilgrims' joints and feet, good meals to fuel their bodies, and comfortable beds, all seasoned with engaging discussions about God and our place in this world. We were missional geniuses.

Naturally, planning such an albergue can't really start until both of us had walked the Way of Saint James together, and my friend had never done so. That meant we needed to plan a trip. We were going to walk the Camino and scout out prime locations for the albergue while I wrote a book on loving your neighbor. Our wives and kids would come along and stay in Airbnb's along the route so that we could see them as we hiked. The plan was foolproof. All we had to do was convince our wives, and that turned out to be a lot easier than we expected. We set a date and began telling friends about it. Before long, we had managed to convince a few other people to join us. It was going to be awesome.

Then, six months before the trip, James decided he was going to take a sports medicine fellowship, which meant that he could not come on the trip. So much for the entrepreneurial venture. With his wife, therefore, not coming either, that left Hannah basically taking care of our kids by herself in a foreign country, and she was not excited about that at all. Yet, when she decided she didn't want to go and I tried to drop out as well, she told me I shouldn't.

"It wouldn't be right for you to back out," she pressed. "You really want to do this and you've convinced everyone to walk with you."

Crap, man. This sucks.

A month away from my wife and kids didn't sound appealing at all, not to mention all the people who were immediately going to judge me. "You're going to leave your wife and kids for a whole month and go on a vacation?" I could hear the condescending tones already. I found myself at an impasse. I wanted to go, but at the same time I didn't want to leave my family. Hannah and I went back and forth for a while before she convinced me that I should go, saying she wanted to give it to me as a gift.

How many wives give their husbands a Camino? So, I decided to buy my ticket, realizing that my Camino had already changed before it even started.

Proverbs 16:9 says, "In their hearts humans plan their course, but the Lord establishes their steps." Putting this trip together made me realize those words were far truer than I imagined. I was convinced to purchase my ticket through my friend, Roshelle, one of the people who was going to be walking the Camino with me. Roshelle is driven and capable, and if she isn't knowledgeable in any particular area, she is going to study, learn, and work hard until she is. She's a smart person and, despite what she believes about herself, wears her heart on her sleeve. She also had the foresight prior to the Camino to get a business credit card that gave her good deals on airlines.

So, with the idea of saving money in mind, I grabbed my laptop and sat down with her and Kelly after church to plan the exact dates and flights we were going to take. Kelly was going with us because she was compelled by the relationships she felt she could form while there. She loves people and has the odd ability to be extremely sarcastic and loving at the same time. People are drawn to Kelly like flies to honey because they can sense she genuinely loves them the moment she sees them.

I really wanted to fly into Bilbao, Spain, and take a shared taxi to Saint Jean. Roshelle wanted to fly into Bilbao and spend the next day there before making our way to Saint Jean. I didn't want to stall. I knew that I'd have a hard time relaxing in Bilbao with my focus on getting underway. I'm walking the Camino, not exploring the Guggenheim, I thought sardonically. But my book is going to be on loving my neighbor, and Roshelle really wants to see it.

Then there was Dan. He was my third companion and wanted to spend the day in Bilbao as well, so I relented and went along with spending the extra day there. Dan is a little taller than I am, at about six feet, with a scruffy beard and a few art degrees. He's one of those guys who is uncomfortable to talk to at times because you can't figure out if what he just said was awkward or brilliant. I usually defer to the idea that he is just trying to help me understand the complex realities of life, mind, and experience, and how they all converge. Dan's cool.

We bought our tickets and made our plans. Kelly and I would drive to Phoenix together and grab a flight to London from there. Roshelle would meet us in London because she wanted to first visit some family in California. Dan would meet us in Bilbao, flying in for just two weeks because he needed to get back for work.

A month prior to our departure date, Tabitha decided she wanted to go. She is quiet and is a mystery to most people. She connects deeply with you, cares about you, asks intriguing questions, and listens, but you spend so much time answering and sharing about yourself that you tend to forget to ask her about what's happening in her life. Bridget jumped in as well. She was ready for a break from working with Intervarsity Christian Fellowship at the University of Arizona. She spent much of her career trying to teach college students about Jesus without taking any vacations. The time for a sabbatical was well past due, so she planned to join us for the last few weeks of the Camino and do some other traveling afterward.

When it was time to go, Kelly arrived at my house so we could drive together to the airport. Leaving was difficult. Like a Band-Aid, you don't look forward to ripping it off but do it quickly to lessen the sting. I kissed Hannah and my daughters, Rosie and Clara, goodbye, jumped in the truck, backed out, and looked in the rearview mirror at everyone waving goodbye. Then, knowing there was no point lingering in the awkwardness and avoidance of the pain, I pulled away fast, already missing them as I hit the gas.

Halfway to the airport, Kelly looked at me. "You doing okay?" she asked gently.

"Yeah, it'll be fine." I'd hardly said a word, and she must've picked up that I was thinking about them. "I'm gonna miss them, but that's just going to have to be a part of my journey this time."

The flight to London was an overnighter, so I was hoping to get a few hours of shut eye before we arrived. Fat chance. Sleeping on a plane sucks even though the seat reclines a luxurious three inches. I did that dumb looking thing people do when they fall asleep sitting up. My eyes slowly closed, my muscles relaxed, and I immediately jerked up as my head plummeted forward toward my chest. Looking about the cabin, I saw other heads bobbing up and down in the same whiplash routine. At times my tailbone hurt so much that I stood up and did some calf stretches before sitting down to curse the guy who invented such unyielding seat cushions. The flight, all nine-and-a-half hours of it, was not great.

London Heathrow Airport is a sentient being—and it hates me. London Heathrow Airport also hates Kelly. Years earlier, Kelly and I had gone through there on a mission trip to Ireland. During a layover, security agents needlessly searched and questioned me, and they almost didn't let Kelly through the passport line because the security person thought for some reason or another that she was trying to stay in England. We were detained so long we almost missed our connecting flight to the Emerald Isle. We were stopped, searched, and questioned again on the return trip. I must look like a terrorist or something.

Sure enough, when we got off the plane this time we rounded toward security, deciding to stop on the way and find the gate number for our connecting flight. It wasn't on the screen. Puzzled, we went up to the airline counter, where the guy took our tickets and passports, clicked around on the computer for a few minutes, and then nonchalantly announced, "That flight doesn't exist."

"What do you mean it doesn't exist?" I asked cheerily, hoping my upbeat tone might make him more inclined to help us.

"That flight doesn't exist," he repeated as he handed back the passports and tickets. "We only have a morning flight to Bilbao and the one on your tickets is for the afternoon."

"So, what do we do? It existed when we bought our tickets," Kelly replied, definitely not trying to sound cheery.

The phone rang and he answered it, basically blowing us off, so we found someone else who also informed us the flight didn't exist. He explained that it was only a seasonal flight, adding that we could not fix it without the credit card attached to the confirmation number. Problem was, Roshelle had the card, so we were trapped waiting for her, and the miraculous credit card that saved us a little money on a non-existent flight, before we could proceed toward security.

London Heathrow Airport hates us.

An hour-and-a-half later, Roshelle found us waiting for her. We filled her in and approached the airline counter again. This time, a new guy was behind it, and he booked us new tickets. That was great, except that they were for a different airport, Gatwick Airport, because Heathrow didn't have any more flights out until the next day.

London has five airports—and I'm pretty sure they all hate us.

We finally got on our flight. Kelly was seated next to me, and Roshelle was across the aisle several rows back. Since London to Bilbao was just a few hours, I bought a cup of coffee before boarding. I wasn't going to sleep on the flight, and I figured the coffee would help avoid the head bobbing ritual.

It didn't. Halfway through the flight I nodded off, holding the coffee between my legs with my right hand on top of the lid. Suddenly, I felt like I was free falling through the air and jolted awake. At the same time, all my muscles tensed, my legs squeezed the cup, and coffee went streaming all over my crotch, onto the seat, and down toward my butt. I looked around, dazed. Kelly, her eyes wide with shock, whispered loudly, "What happened?"

"I must have fallen asleep," I foolishly replied, glad the coffee wasn't hot anymore. Then we burst out in uncontrollable laughter. I looked back at Roshelle. She was sound asleep and had missed the whole thing.

Across the aisle from us sat a guy in his early fifties with a black button-up shirt and nice dress shoes. He obviously had no sense of humor because he just scowled at us. For a second, I thought maybe I should try and compose myself. Planes are kind of like libraries, and I felt like we'd violated some no-noise policy. Then I looked at him again and realized I really didn't care what he thought. There are a lot of people who have forgotten how to express joy. They're too stuffy, too arrogant. It's pride that often prevents us from having a good hearty laugh by telling us such behavior is foolish. I decided I'd rather laugh and look like an idiot than be like the guy in the button-up shirt.

As I leaned up to hit the call button for a flight attendant, I looked down to see that my leather seat was drenched in a sea of caffeine. The attendant brought a few napkins, and I became painfully aware that it looked like I had peed my pants. With no way of covering up, I waddled to the front of the plane to get more napkins to take care of the soaked seat.

Stuffy guy just stared at me as I returned. Kelly chuckled. I smiled.

After drying the seat, I knew I was just going to get soaked again when I sat down. My pants had sponged up about half of the ocean of liquid as it was. So, I was off again, this time to the lavatory. Airplane bathrooms are tiny and usually pretty gross. It's almost like people forget how to use the restroom when they're on a plane. Gratefully, this one was pretty clean. As I used the paper towels to dry my pants, my elbows kept smashing against the walls. I could only imagine what people outside were thinking as they heard the muffled banging sounds on the walls of the compartment.

I laughed again. They'll have a good story to tell.

We landed in Bilbao a little after 11:00 p.m. and grabbed an Uber whose driver must've been running from the cops. Roshelle and I slid around in the back seat and glanced at each other whenever we thought we were going to die, which was often. Kelly sat in the front and complimented the driver for not going slowly. Kelly is apparently secure in the fact that she's going to heaven. I'm sure of it, too, but I still had a family to get back to.

In no time, we were dropped off near an alley where our Airbnb was we mercifully ushered ourselves out of the car. Kelly chatted quickly the ride was while Roshelle and I looked at her in We started looking for the address, and Roshelle texted Tabitha, who had arrived earlier, so that she could meet us at the entrance. The door was worn, and instead of a normal knob, it had a huge metal ball in the center. We clunkily made our way through it into a small stairwell. Our packs shuffled back and forth scraping against the walls. We weren't used to them yet, but in a few days, I knew they'd feel like such a part of our bodies it would seem weird whenever we took them off.

Dan was already there, too, and was pumped that we'd finally arrived. We decided where we were all going to sleep. Dan and I took the living room, while the girls shared the bedroom. I wasn't tired anymore, so Dan and Roshelle joined me and we went out to explore. Bilbao was beautiful at night. I had no clue where I was in the city and my coffee butt was still damp, but I was comfortable and happy. After a few hours we walked back into the Airbnb and decided to get some shut eye.

The Guggenheim opened in 1997 and changed the fate of the once decaying city. Bilbao was a booming industrial city until the 1970s when area companies couldn't keep up with technological advances. It declined until Frank Gehry, with the strong backing of city officials, built the Guggenheim. They realized it could draw art lovers from thousands of miles away, and they were right. The building itself is a work of art and is filled with pieces from noted neo-conceptual artist Jenny Holzer to pop art icon Andy Warhol.

Roshelle was excited to see the Guggenheim because she is an architect and loves all things nerdy and mathematical. Dan has more art degrees than should be humanly possible, so he was stoked to check out the different displays of work and revel in their glory. Kelly, Tabitha, and I were really just along for the ride, and the line outside reminded me of waiting to go on one, though I was impressed by the sheer scope of the place.

Once inside, we split up and began to look around. The first room I entered was filled with several huge, brown, walled-in hallways that you could walk through. I assumed they would lead to something, but they didn't. The first one I meandered through featured two wavy walls that led straight out the other end. The second was a spiral where I had to maneuver around other people to get to nothing in the center of it. The third had two straight, brown walls that could've been any hallway in the world.

I have no clue why this is art, I mused. These are just walls. Walls that lead nowhere.

I left that area, looking for something more -- well, purposeful -- and came upon some vertical scrolling marquees with messages that were encouraging? Depressing? They were so non-sensical I couldn't tell. Whatever the marquees were supposed to be, they didn't seem like art to me either, and when they were followed by a bunch of paint drippings on canvas, I decided I was done. Maybe I'm uncultured or a redneck or something, but I just don't get modern art. Kelly and Tabitha were apparently thinking the same thing as we ran into one another near the same exit. We agreed to leave, grab a coffee, and trek the city instead of working our way through the tourists in the Guggenheim to stare at things we didn't understand.

Bilbao is filled with fountains, courtyards, and centuries-old buildings. We walked through the streets for a few hours looking at statues and dodging traffic until we figured it was time to head back so we could snag our taxi to Saint Jean. Roshelle and Dan met me at the exit from the Guggenheim and were shocked that I had left. "I mean, it's the freakin' Guggenheim!" Roshelle exclaimed in disgust. "It's world famous!"

"The building is cool," I explained as we climbed the stairs to street-level, "but the art didn't make any sense."

"I could have explained it all to you if you would have asked," Dan exclaimed.

"But here's the thing. I just don't really care that much about art." Even as the words left my mouth, I realized I had just downplayed my friend's deepest passion. Everyone went quiet.

What an idiot.

We had to take a bus back to where the taxi was going to pick us up, and thanks to my foolish tongue, the ride was a little awkward. The girls chatted about this and that, but Dan and I just stood there in silence until I got the nerve to apologize. "Don't worry about it," he said, his voice upbeat. "It's no big deal. Some people like art and some don't."

The mood was back to normal as we caught our taxi and made our way to Saint Jean. We arrived before the pilgrim's office closed, so we decided to get our passports. The lady behind the desk took my information, gave me my passport, and then added, "You can't go the Napoleon route. There was a storm yesterday, and they shut it down. You'll have to take the Charlemagne route tomorrow instead."

I tried to hide my disappointment. My guidebook said the Napoleon route is considered the official French way to begin the Camino and goes straight up the mountain before descending at the end. It was the same route Hannah and I took the first time. It had a myriad of different trails, roads, and scenery. The Charlemagne route follows a road the majority of the time, leaving you avoiding traffic for most of the day. That's fine," I responded, knowing the others were listening. I didn't want them to feel bad for me.

We left the office, found our albergue, set our packs by our beds, and wandered the streets looking for a restaurant. Every place looked closed, but we were directed to a main street where we found a restaurant filled with pilgrims. As we dined, we talked about the beginning of our Camino. Since I was the only one who had read the guidebook, I explained what the Charlemagne route was going to be like. "The beginning is pretty flat, followed by an easy incline until just before the end, and then that last part is hellacious," I told them. "It's basically straight up, but it leads to the same albergue in Roncesvailles as the

Napoleon route."

We also discussed what we were hoping to learn about ourselves, God, and one another. Dan and I didn't have a clue what to expect, but each of the girls had something she was working through, and they were praying that the pilgrimage would lead them to a better understanding of the issues. Mostly, though, we talked about the basics. Everyone had a lot of questions, and since I had already walked the Camino, I spent most of the time talking.

"On a pilgrimage you have one responsibility, and that is to take care of your body, so bring water. Always have water. You need water to survive, and I can't tell you how many people I've come across on the trail who had none." I suppose my memory of Hannah's dehydration last time was utmost in my mind, but I chose not to share that story. "Secondly, carry a few snacks because you're going to get hungry, and you'll need it to fuel your body. Take care of your feet, too. Those things are going to take the brunt of your weight, plus the weight of your pack, for five hundred miles. They're gonna blister up like crazy in the beginning, but if you take care of your feet, they'll turn into nicely calloused machines."

Next, I recommended that they make sure their packs were not too heavy and fit just right. "A heavy, off-kilter pack will rub your back or shoulders raw, and it could lead to all sorts of tendon issues. Adjust your pack if it's causing any problems," I said. "Lastly, don't be nervous. Just put one foot in front of the other. It'll be hard, and you'll feel like quitting, but put that next foot out anyway. The Camino is a challenge, and it's through that challenge that you grow in your understanding of yourself and God. You never really know what you're going to experience until you actually walk it, and then you realize that you really have no control at all. This pilgrimage throws a lot of surprises at you."

As we walked back to the albergue, I thought about how this Camino had already surprised me. After all, I'd made my original plans, only to see everything change. Now, as I accepted the fact that I was even going to be taking a different initial route than I hoped, I couldn't help but wonder what other unexpected surprises awaited me.

I'm excited to find out. I think.

OUR ALBERGUE SEPARATED THE MEN'S SLEEPING QUARTERS FROM THE women's. The ladies were on the main floor while the men had to go outside and climb a set of stairs to get to the second floor of the building. The room Dan and I were in had two parallel bunk beds with about three feet of space between them. I didn't mind the lack of room, but what did bother me was that the bottom bunks were occupied. I hate sleeping on the top bunk because every move you make shakes the whole thing. So, when I sleep on the top, I try not to move too much, but I get so focused on not moving that I never really feel comfortable. Then there's the whole going-to-the-bathroom-in-the-middle-of-the-night thing, which I remembered all too well from the first Camino when I scraped my shin on the ladder while trying to get down without waking Hannah.

I spent the night in and out of sleep. I was jet lagging pretty hard, understandable with the nine-hour difference between Saint Jean and Tucson. I tried to will myself asleep, dozed off, and then found myself wide awake once again. At one point, my left arm had fallen asleep, so when I rolled over it flopped onto my chest like a dead fish. In my delirium, I thought someone had smacked me, so I grabbed it with my other arm and flung it off as hard as I could. It smacked into the wall with a loud thunk, and my arm felt as though it was being prodded by a thousand needles.

I quickly jerked up to see if I had awakened anyone. Nope. It was just me. I checked my watch hoping it was close to the morning, saw it was not close at all, and lay back down.

Four in the morning is not usually when I like to start my day because I'm not a crazy person, but that's precisely when I decided to give up and head over to the breakfast area. The hospitalero told us he didn't lock it up at night because people usually liked to get an early start. I grabbed my Bible and journal, figuring I could spend some time reading, writing, and praying while sipping some coffee.

For the next hour and a half, not a single soul entered that room. Apparently, I was the only one who couldn't sleep. I was thankful for it, though, because it gave me alone time to consider the next few days. The beginning can set the tone for the rest of the journey. How many miles you walk a day, your pace, where you take breaks, or whom you connect with can determine what kind of group joins you or if you walk alone. Your mindset going in can cause you to quit or push on. A lot of people start in less-than-great shape and end up injuring themselves or having to take a few day's rest. The beginning of the Camino is important.

Knowing that, I talked to Jesus and wrote in my journal. As I did, I realized that my beginning was going to be marked by two vital factors. First, I had promised both Kelly and Tabitha that I would walk with them. They were both nervous about the trek up the mountain to Roncevailles, and I knew the temptation to quit then would be a huge one. There was no doubt they could do it, but I also understood that sometimes you don't think you can and need a friend to lean on. I was absolutely determined to be that friend and make sure they got up that mountain no matter what. I'd carry their packs or give them my water. Heck, I'd pull them up in a wagon if I had to.

The second thing was to get to that stream where Hannah wanted to dip her feet. For some reason, that moment of failure to love my wife haunted me. I'd made a ton of mistakes in my marriage, and most of them were worked out and we moved on. But this was different. I needed to get to that stream, put my feet in, and have a moment. I didn't know what kind of moment it was going to be. I just knew I had to do it.

When the other pilgrims finally started filtering into the breakfast area, I began to really feel the anticipation of the Camino's first day. Sipping my coffee, I closed my books and started eavesdropping on the different conversations. I couldn't understand most of them because they were in different languages: German, Korean, Dutch, Spanish, and others that I couldn't identify at all. The communal table is the most diverse and unifying place on earth. Some people spoke with a hectic speed while others kept a slow, steady cadence. Most whispered like they were in a library, but all gulped down their coffee and breakfast with urgency. They were ready to get on the trail.

By the time our crew assembled, the sun was barely up, but most everyone else was already on their way. In the beginning, pilgrims begin walking earlier than necessary. As they get used to the routine, they start sleeping in a little more. Quite frankly, I wasn't worried about everyone leaving before us because there was a good chance many were going to quit before they got to the end of that day's walk. We would definitely get a bed in the albergue. I slowly got my pack ready, making sure the heavy items were placed close to my back on the hip straps with the lighter items surrounding them. When I finished, I hoisted the beast on my back and headed to see if everyone else was ready.

They weren't. So, I took off the pack and sat down with another cup of joe hoping we could get the show on the road before too long. My attitude was so different from the first Camino with Hannah. I was in such a hurry then. I knew better now, and that knowledge gave me patience and allowed me to better enjoy the moment. One by one, my friends gradually assembled their packs and were ready to take on the first path up the mountain. We were nervous and excited, but no one talked about it.

It was only then I realized that I had completely disregarded one of my rules: taking care of my feet. I learned on my first Camino that my feet did well when I rubbed Vaseline all over them, then put on a sock liner before putting on my socks. The darn ritual saved me after nearly two weeks of blisters so bad they engulfed my right pinky toe. It literally disappeared under a series of pustules that compounded one on top of the other. I couldn't even see my toenail. It looked like a fat, fleshy marshmallow. Then someone suggested Vaseline. After that, there were no more blisters.

"I forgot to Vaseline my feet," I told the group, annoyed with myself. "You guys should hit the road, though. I'll catch up." Kelly and Tabitha decided to get started since they figured they'd be slower. Dan realized he'd made the same mistake I did, and Roshelle figured she'd just wait for us. That didn't stop her from whipping out her camera and taking pictures of everything around her while Dan and I slathered our feet with the semi-liquid goo.

When we finally got underway, we maintained a solid clip. My watch told me we were pacing at about 4.3 miles per hour, and I was extra attentive to catch all the markers along the route. I wanted to make sure we weren't going to get lost. It took us about a half an hour to catch up to Kelly and Tabitha, which impressed me because they didn't leave that long before us. They were going faster than I thought they would. Once we met up, I slowed down to walk with them as Dan and Roshelle sped ahead.

I had planned to follow the same "jerk, stall, repeat" method with Kelly and Tabitha that I used with Hannah, minus the frustration I allowed myself to feel the first time. As I began the routine, I chatted with the girls a bit before speeding ahead, and then I stopped and waited as they caught up, making sure to give them an encouraging word when they did. It was working great until a giant Swede caught up with me and started talking to me. We exchanged the usual conversation—"What's your name?" "Where are you from?" "Why are you walking?" Yada yada

yada—until he said something that caught my attention.

"I hope we make it in before the storm hits." He was upbeat and cheerful about it, but I was a little perplexed. Back at the pilgrim's office, we were told nothing about the potential of bad weather.

"There's a storm coming?" I asked. "What time is it going to hit?"

"Four o'clock," he replied, shock in his voice. He was obviously surprised I didn't know about it. "My weather app warned me this morning."

I considered the pace Kelly and Tabitha were making and concluded we were going to cut it close. Walking in a storm is never fun, so we were going to have to start pushing a little harder. I said goodbye to the Swede and decided to stop and wait for the girls to catch up so I could let them know what was happening.

When they arrived, before I could say anything, Kelly let me know that Tabitha had forgotten her water.

I thought back to what I had told them the night before.

I thought back to what happened with Hannah the last time.

She forgot her water? Son of a gun!

I intuitively used my Christian swear words instead of what I actually wanted to say.

"I've been sharing mine with her," Kelly said, sounding pretty confident nothing was the matter. "She's been sipping from mine when she needs a drink."

I took a breath and figured there had to be a ton of places to fill up on water along the route. Maybe it wouldn't be a big deal at all.

Turned out the Charlemagne route had exactly zero places to fill up water.

Zeeeeerrrroooo plaaaaaacccces!

I told them about the storm coming at four o'clock and gently pushed them to move a little faster. After a while, something hit Tabitha, and she began moving faster than she had done all day. It was like something in her snapped, and she just decided to get up the freakin' mountain. She bolted ahead while Kelly and I limped along.

Jerk. Stall. Repeat. The rhythm started wearing on me the more I thought about the coming storm.

When people are exhausted, they react to things differently. I should've known that, because Hannah's coping ability was stopping and crying while mine was putting my nose to the grindstone and make it work.

Kelly's reaction to exhaustion was to hike for a bit, then stop, lay down, and stare at the sky.

A storm is rolling in, I thought, and she is laying down.

"Hey, you doing alright?" I asked, trying to repress any trace of annoyance in my voice.

"I'm exhausted. I need a break," she pled, trying to catch her breath. "Can I have a drink of your water?"

I handed her the hose connected to the water bladder I carried in my pack. "Okay, we'll break for a little bit. But there's a storm coming, and we don't want to get caught in it." I figured she would be good to go after a not-too-long rest, and I sat down next to her. I don't know if I have an abnormally small butt or something, but I could not find a comfortable position. No matter what I did, something jabbed into me. After what seemed like 20 minutes, but was really a lot less, I got up and rubbed off my sore rump. "We should hit the road."

Kelly rose, and we continued on. It was clear she was struggling, and I felt really bad for her. I wanted to help her beat this first obstacle. On the other hand, we were not moving fast at all with so many little breaks, and she didn't seem to have any urgency about the impending storm. I needed to find a way to actively encourage her so that we could each move forward with the right mindset.

I decided to try what my dad used to do to me when he hauled me up all sorts of rugged mountain trails when I was a kid. I hiked ahead and stopped on top of a hill. "This is it, Kelly. You just need to get here, and then we'll take another break. You're doing great. You're killing it!" I did all I could to sound excited so that she could hear how much I believed in her despite my growing frustration. It helped because I had something to focus on. When she reached me, we sipped from my water and rested before repeating the process.

About four miles out from the Roncesvailles, I ran out of water. This is not good, I reasoned, but it's not terrible. It could be worse. Then I thought, Of course, this wouldn't be a problem if we could move at my pace. I think a snail just passed me. I corrected myself. I gotta get it together. We need to get up this mountain.

"This is not a great situation, Kelly. We really need to start going faster." I hoped she caught the urgency in my voice.

She did, but not the way I wanted. "I'm going as fast as I can," she whined sharply. I had obviously crossed a line.

"Sorry," I backtracked and resorted back to the earlier encouragement tactic. Meanwhile, we saw fewer people. Most had likely already made it to the albergue. When we did come across someone, Kelly asked for a drink. She got the same reply every time. "I ran out, too."

Don't. Forget. Water.

We trekked on until we were passed by a group of chatty ladies whose accents told me they were American. Kelly stopped them.

"Could I please have a sip of your water?"

One of the ladies, the blonde one, said with a smile on her face, "Oh, sorry. I don't have any." She sounded like a know-it-all.

"I'm not feeling good," Kelly replied. "I think I'm dehydrated."

I looked closer, saw Kelly's face was a little flush, and I was pretty sure she was beginning to get dehydrated, but she wasn't totally there yet.

"You should lie down and put your feet up," Blondie insisted. "That's what I do when I'm tired." She then turned and started hiking on.

It was definitely not the advice I wanted Kelly to hear, but what really bothered me is that as the woman turned to leave, I saw her water bottle. It was half full. She had plenty to share, but she chose not to. I just stared into the back of their heads as they walked away while Kelly again lay down.

I consider myself patient, maybe even more patient than most. I try to let things go. I took a personality test once that told me my self-assumptions were wrong, and I thought it must be right because my level of pissed-off-ness, if that's a word, hit its max. Obscenities twisted through my mind like a whirlwind. I didn't move. I just stood there, stared, and thought of all the things I wanted to say to that blonde, water-hogging liar.

After I calmed down, I turned to Kelly. "That lady had water. I saw it in her pack as she turned to walk away. She's a terrible pilgrim. Pilgrims take care of one another." That seemed a more "pastorly" response than what I'd been thinking moments earlier.

Kelly said nothing. She just struggled to her feet once more. We marched on and caught up to an Italian man sitting and leaning up against a tree. Smoking his cigarette and staring off into space, he looked like he didn't have a care in the world. This guy looks super chill. I hope he has water. I knew Kelly was going to ask. She was pretty desperate.

The dude did—and he shared his water.

Pilgrims take care of one another.

Kelly thanked him profusely and the three of us chatted for a while before I said we needed to push on. A few sprinkles started dropping here and there, but it didn't seem like anything to really worry about yet. The trail led us to the street where a recreational vehicle was parked in a pullout. As we approached it, a dog bounded out of the unlatched screen door. He wasn't huge, but he was big enough, maybe a chocolate Lab, and his bark certainly sounded like it meant business as he flew toward me. Instinctively, I swung my walking staff out toward him, trying to keep some distance between him and us as I shuffled backward. "Whoa! Whoa!" If I had been fully hydrated, I would have peed my pants.

The lady in the R.V. came out slowly walked toward us and called the dog off. "Sorry about that." She didn't seem concerned at all about the situation.

"We're sorry to bother you," Kelly said, "but could you fill up my water bottle?"

"Of course!" She grabbed Kelly's bottle and looked at me. "Do you want any?"

"Nah, I'm fine." Secretly, I wanted some. I probably really needed some, but I had made a comment earlier to Kelly that I really didn't need a lot of water and that she should drink as much of mine as she needed. I was regretting that statement by now, but for some reason my pride got the best of me.

So dumb.

As we got on our way, a somewhat rejuvenated Kelly made fun of me for running from the dog. Mockery is her love language. It made for a badly needed laugh, and she was moving way faster now that she had a good drink. We made good time until the wind picked up. It slowed us down, blew my baseball cap off a few times, and was sometimes so loud I couldn't even hear my own thoughts. It howled for the last hour of our walk, but we pushed through, feeling better because Kelly had her water, and we were getting closer.

We pulled into Roncesvailles just after 4:30 p.m., only to find that the monastery there was packed. While Kelly, infused from all the rehydration, rushed off to the restroom, I spoke with the hospitelaro, a tiny lady with short salt-and-pepper hair and a commanding presence.

"There is no more room!" She sounded stressed out. "You can try the hotel or keep walking."

I looked at her, stunned. Crap. I immediately thought about all of the wasted time, all of the breaks, all of the restraint that I shouldn't have had when I was waiting for Kelly along the path.

If I hadn't waited, I would have a bed.

I would never have even been in this line.

I would have already unpacked my gear and found a comfortable spot to relax.

Then I remembered something from the first Camino, a mantra I heard over and over until it became annoying. "You never know what the Camino has for you." It's funny how irritating sayings often prove to be true. I figured maybe this was something the Camino had for me. God was going to use this hiccup too, I don't know, form me somehow. Make me better. More like Him.

So, instead of freaking out, I decided to chill.

I politely thanked the harried hospitelaro. She looked almost in shock.

"Rough day?" I asked, knowing she had surely already been through the wringer with multiple pilgrims.

"Yeah," she conceded. "There's more pilgrims than there are beds, and we didn't plan for this." With that, she removed any opportunity for me to reply and started giving me directions to the only hotel in the area. As I listened, I looked around at all of the pilgrims standing in line and spotted Tabitha and Roshelle. They walked up to me just as the lady finished her directions. Both of them looked a little worried and asked what I was going to do just as Kelly returned.

"Well, there's only two options," I said. "Keep on walking or pay for the hotel." I figured we could trek on to the next town, which couldn't be any more than a couple of miles away.

"There is no way I am walking to the next town," Kelly stated matter-of-factly, and so, that was that. We briskly walked toward the hotel, knowing that other pilgrims were going to be wanting rooms as well.

Pilgrims take care of one another.

Unless you get to Roncesvailles, and there are no beds left in the albergue. In that case, you grab a room as fast as you can before anyone else can get their grubby little fingers on it.

Yes, at times I am a hypocrite.

We snagged the last room available, a suite with four beds, and found two other pilgrims to share the space and split the room cost with us. Kelly insisted on paying because I had waited for her, and I reluctantly gave her a quiet, appreciative verbal agreement.

Such verbal agreements are different than the ones that go on in your head. The one in my mind went something like, "Sweet! A free room!"

The storm rolled in while Kelly, Roshelle, and I ate dinner and wondered where Dan was. The rain was thick and heavy, and I was grateful the first day was over and that I had done what I set out to do. I made sure Kelly and Tabitha made it through the first day. Now that they had done that, I was confident they'd have no problem getting through the rest of the Camino.

The first day is the most daunting. It can make you want to quit because you realize you have no clue what you got yourself into. You walk up the first freakin' mountain and realize the training you did wasn't enough. You begin to question your mental capability to accomplish all 500 miles. You forget that not all days will be like this because you're caught up in the moment—the pain, the fear of failure, the thirst or hunger. You forget you're on a pilgrimage, a sacred journey meant to be done in remembrance of God. To be walked with Him as you make your way to Santiago to complete your act of worship.

Or maybe you're just taking a walk. Either way, the first day can really suck, so I was glad that it was done as I turned my attention to what I needed to do on tomorrow's journey to the next stop, Zubiri.

Get to that stream.

THE STORM RAGED THROUGH THE NIGHT AND WOKE ME UP A FEW TIMES, but other than that I got a much-needed good night's rest and rose the next morning pretty refreshed. My first thought was that I needed to form a routine, a morning ritual to help me start the day off on the right foot. I packed up my supplies in a hurry, trying to figure out the best way to distribute the weight of the pack, only to end up plopping things into place, removing them, and redistributing them to new parts of the bag. After I finally locked in on what I thought was the best arrangement, I headed outside to meet the crew.

Dan was a quick find, which surprised me since I never located him the night before. He was still gathering some things together before he was set to go. Tabitha, Roshelle, and Kelly were busy either repacking their supplies or getting breakfast.

Knowing I was in for a wait, I ducked underneath an awning as the storm continued to drizzle down. It was the perfect time for me to record my thoughts about all that had happened the day before, and I brought both a journal and a voice recorder to log my experiences and thoughts along the way. I whipped out the recorder, feeling somewhat official as I did, like one of those journalists you see in the movies capturing the audio of an interview or a detective working on a case he's about to crack while taking a drag from a cigarette. However, my thoughts ended up being few and far between. It took a mere two minutes to recount the entire first day, and I couldn't think of much else to say. So, I put the machine in my pocket and decided to lean against the wall and watch all of the other pilgrims depart as I waited for my friends.

I was too distracted, too preoccupied with what the day's primary task could bring.

Be patient, I reminded myself. They'll be ready soon.

So, I paced back and forth, coming up with excuses for why it was taking so long for everyone to get their stuff together so we could hit the road. After a long 15 minutes, we gathered together in our little pilgrim cluster and began our journey.

The rain was still coming down as we took our first steps and crossed the road to the trail, skidding a bit on the mud. Because we had already crested the mountain, the weather didn't concern me as much as it had the day before when I found out the storm was coming. I also knew more trees were on the trail ahead to protect us from the rain, not to mention a lot more towns along the way. Still, I mused about the enormous task in front of us. Day One is down. Now we just have to walk the rest of this beast, starting with today's trek to Zubiri. I strived to turn my thoughts positive. We are together, and we are going to help and support one another through the pain and the trial.

And wait for one another.

In no time I outpaced the group and ended up a good 30 yards ahead of everyone.

Hmm. Today's gonna be rough. I leaned on my staff and watched them smile and chat as they inched toward me. They were genuinely happy, carefree even, while I stood there grousing that the last thing I wanted to do was to spend the day waiting on them to catch up.

I did that yesterday. Today is about getting to that stream, not waiting.

By the time the group caught up to me, I had already decided to suggest they were ready to walk on their own. They really didn't need me.

They had finished the first day. Now they just had to keep putting one foot in front of the other. As I was wondering how they'd respond to that, Tabitha interrupted my thoughts. "Hey, Nick, you don't have to wait for us."

"Yeah, you waited all day for us yesterday," Kelly chimed in. "We're fine, go ahead."

"Are you sure?" I asked, hoping I sounded more hesitant than I really felt. I was instantly excited to go ahead on my own, but I also felt guilty. I shouldn't be so impatient. I shouldn't want to do my own thing. I should want to walk with the group.

But I really didn't want to. Not today.

"Okay, let's all meet up in Zubiri then," I said, already turning away so I could get going.

The group responded with a quick, enthusiastic "yeah," and I hit the trail.

Hiking in the rain is one of my least favorite things to do. I've always thought those love scenes in movies where the couple dances and kisses in the rain are pretty stupid. The essential problem with rain is that it makes you wet. Yup, huge scientific discovery: rain equals wet. To avoid the wet, of course, you put on a rain jacket, but it just traps heat against your body. As you keep the jacket on and begin to sweat, you become even wetter. You can't win.

I trod ahead, unzipping the jacket so it could vent a little, but I got wet from both the rain and my sweat.

I don't like hiking in the rain.

It continued to drizzle as I sloshed through the muck from the trails and stomped it off whenever I periodically hit some pavement. But, I told myself, I was walking at my own pace and, therefore, was able to explore the towns I encountered. The first had a Catholic church with a plaque outside that proudly declared how members used to hold witch trials there and burn the offenders alive at a stake in the nearby forest.

Church history is crazy. People suck. I thought it was insane what people could do to one another and how they could destroy anything. Jesus said the two greatest commandments are to love God with your whole being and love one another. Love God. Love Others. Yet somehow people took those two commandments and said, "Yeah, we should burn witches." What the deuce!

I was positively antsy as I arrived at Zubiri in the early afternoon. I had made good time, really good time, clocking in at over four miles per hour on average. I might as well have been jogging the whole time. But I couldn't have slowed down. I was too driven. I had to put my feet in that stream. I needed to do it for Hannah—or was it really for Hannah? I wasn't sure if she even really cared if I did it or not.

No. I was doing this for myself.

I needed to shed some guilt and a lot of shame. After all, I'd been carrying them around all day up to that point.

The bridge from the trail to the town of Zubiri was filled with pilgrims looking over the side and into the water. Some were talking. More than a few were crying. That's weird, I thought as I passed. Today wasn't really a hard day. Why are they crying? Usually, tears are shed if the hiking has been tough, but despite the rain, I believed the trekking had been easy.

Regardless of my curiosity, I brushed off what was going on around me as I peered over the right side of the bridge to look at the bank where I wanted to put my feet into the water. It was the precise spot where Hannah and I were the last time we were here. There was no one near the edge.

Good. I'll have time to sit and think without a million people around me.

I finished crossing the bridge and decided to first go to a little café where I grabbed a ham sandwich and an orange soda. For some reason, I crave either orange soda or Coca Cola when I hike. I normally don't drink soda. It's not really good for you, and it makes my stomach feel bloated. But when I take a long hike, maybe it's something to do with the sugar or carbs, or perhaps I simply have an innate need to undo the benefits of the exercise I just did. I just need to have one. Either way, I took my food and the soda, headed back to the stream, dropped my pack on the ground, and sat down.

The expectation of the moment was crushed as soon as I took off my raincoat. It was freezing. I didn't realize how much heat the jacket had trapped next to my body until the chill in the misty air hit me. My sweat-soaked shirt reminded me why I live in the desert rather than the tundra. I hate being cold, and nothing is colder than a wet shirt being blown against your skin by an icy breeze.

I instantly put the jacket back on, snagged my pack and food, and moved away from the stream to a wall that promised a little protection from the blowing cold. The sun had shown itself a few times earlier, so I decided to eat and wait for the sun to come out before heading back over to put my feet in the water. I'm not going to deal with my shame when I'm cold, I reasoned. I can wait for the perfect moment.

When you have a thought like that, realize it is stupid. The perfect moment never comes. The drizzle never let up, and the chilly wind never turned warm. I just sat there, cold, wet, and eavesdropping on the pilgrims lingering on the bridge.

That, too, was not smart. Before long I heard a particularly distraught pilgrim frantically tell her friends how the albergue in Zubiri was closed and all the extra rooms and hotels were full. She then declared that the next town, Larrasoaña, was already packed with pilgrims. "There's no place to sleep until you get to Pamplona," she proclaimed, "and that's 15 miles away."

After listening to the frantic lady ramble on about how terrible this or that was and how her Camino was completely ruined, I returned to the café to see if her complaints were true. People can tend to exaggerate when they are in a stressful situation, and I doubted her information anyway because of the way she was freaking out.

I was wrong. She was right.

"There's nothing until Pamplona," confirmed the woman behind the counter. She had a cool neck tattoo of a sparrow holding a ribbon in its beak that said something in Spanish. "You should get walking or call a taxi."

Crap, man.

I could do neither of the things she recommended because my friends hadn't arrived yet and would be lost and confused if I just left. There was no way I could contact them because I was the only one with a European phone plan.

What the heck do I do?

You never know what the Camino has for you.

I'll wait. It'll all work out. Besides, you have a stream to get to.

I went back to the wall to dodge the breeze and drizzle. I sat for another hour listening to pilgrims talk about the lack of beds, make calls for taxis, or discuss varying ways to deal with the situation. It kept raining and stayed cold.

So, right where I sat by the wall, I finally prayed.

God, I am sorry that I let my insecurity and fear stop me from letting Hannah put her feet into the stream. I'm sorry that I'm controlled by so many things other than my love for you and for others. Help me to be free to be what you want me to be. Thank you for Hannah. Thank you for giving me someone who is so quick to forgive me. Help me to be better at loving her and you.

That was it. It was so simple—and yet I felt so free.

Heading back to the café, I smirked and then outright chuckled. I was so intent on putting my feet in the water when I all needed to do was to be honest with what I was feeling and thank God for what He gave me.

Wet feet don't solve heart issues. Genuine prayer does.

Now I was ready to officially start my Camino. I had finished the two things I promised myself to do. What else did this Camino have for me?

What was the next day's journey going to bring? How was God going to reveal Himself to me in a new way?

And what kind of beer did the café have? I wanted a beer—a nice dark, heavy beer to sip until my friends arrived.

The café didn't have any stout on tap, but it did have a beer called "Ambar" which, according to the lady with the sparrow tattoo, apparently won some awards in 2016. I figured she'd had to answer a ton of beer questions because pilgrims with different tastes come to her from all over the world, so she must know quite a lot—or not give a rip at all. Either way, that was the beer she suggested, and that's what I selected.

As she poured me a glass from the tap, I looked around from my vantage point at the bar and saw troubled faces all around me discussing the dilemma of the day. How would everyone find beds? One lady with short gray hair was making a big fuss. She was apparently discouraged by the amount of pilgrims walking the Camino, convinced that commercialism had overtaken the event. She accusingly glared at the others at her table, seeing them as the problem because a movie had made the journey famous and they were now here en masse looking for a thrill.

She was right to a certain extent. The number of pilgrims had increased dramatically since Emilio Estevez released his movie about it called The Way. It was a good movie, the same one Hannah watched when she decided to ask me to walk the Camino with her. During that first trek together, we talked with a lot of people who were there because the movie inspired them.

But does commercialism actually ruin the Camino? Does it mean some pilgrims who are better than others? Are some walking for the "wrong" reasons because they are self-centered and only looking for adventure rather than a spiritual experience?

Sure—and that is absolutely no different from the motives of pilgrims in times past. A month after my first Camino, I walked into a

Tucson coffee shop, and the barista asked me what I had been up to lately. She had no clue who I was and probably didn't actually care what was going on in my life, but I decided to tell her I had just walked across Spain.

"Oh, yeah, I started but didn't finish," she said. "It's so commercialized. I just couldn't deal with all of the people. I didn't want to waste my time on it." Her tone suggested she felt she was clearly better than me. She quit because there were too many people, and since I had continued and finished the trek, I was the problem. I suggested she should have finished because the crowd thins out after the first few days. She didn't reply and our conversation ended.

After she handed me my coffee, I realized she was the type of person who wasn't going to do what everyone else did. She was unique. I assumed she was arrogant and I was better than her because I finished what I started. I was more capable. I had the physical, mental, and spiritual attitude to get through it. Besides, I was not at all arrogant. I was humble, probably the most humble person I know. I was proud of that. Super. Proud.

What fools we both were. Maybe still are.

That conversation left a mark on me. People (myself included) will judge others based on anything. I thought about it all again as I sat there with my award-winning beer listening to people worry and complain about the lack of beds. The brew was good, with a medium roasted malt that left me feeling refreshed. Usually Guinness is on the light side for me. I like my beer to make me feel like I just finished a meal, but in this case, "Pilgrim Nick" was enjoying a medium beer. Who'da thought?

The sun popped in and out for another hour before Roshelle arrived. She was famished and ordered some food and a drink. We sat and chatted about who we thought was going to make it to Zubiri first: Kelly, Tabitha, or Dan. Kelly and Tabitha walked in less than an hour later, causing both of us to lose our bets. They were happy, hungry, and excited to tell us about their day. They talked about what they saw, the people they talked to, and the blisters they acquired. But only one thought circled around in my head.

Where the crap is Dan?

He was in better shape and had a quicker pace than I, and should have beaten me to Zubiri. Where was he?

I started to worry he had gotten injured along the way, but then he arrived with a smile on his face and tales about all the cool side routes he took to visit monasteries and statues I never heard of. He'd seen things no one else had—and as he told us about it, I realized he was pursuing what he loved. Dan was passionate about church history, art, and architecture, and he spent the day chasing after those things.

Dan pursued what he loved. I had accomplished a mission.

I was driven by duty and guilt. He was driven by love.

I'm ready for a change of perspective.

Pilgrims slowly drifted away, and we eventually turned our conversation to the "bed" problem. What it boiled down to was that Zubiri's main albergue was under renovation, and a big cycling race happening was at the same time we were there. With all the extra rooms and hotels booked, we chose to take a taxi to Pamplona and then backtrack the next day. We could still walk the whole thing by taking a taxi back to Zubiri the next morning. Not a big deal.

We got someone at the café to call a taxi for us, only to watch it be swarmed and taken by other pilgrims upon its arrival. We called another one, and it happened again and then a third time. We were all frustrated, but Roshelle and Kelly jumped on finding an Airbnb in Pamplona to make sure we had a place to stay when we finally got there—if we ever did.

We commandeered a taxi of our own around 6:00 p.m., which is pretty late for pilgrims searching for a place to stay. Thankfully, we had locked in an Airbnb, so we jumped into the cab with no worries and started talking about our plans for the next day. Everyone had different ideas on when they wanted to get up, especially Kelly. She likes to sleep in and blame it on laziness, though as a late riser myself I see it as an act of freedom and rebellion at the same time. Those pilgrims who get up freakishly early usually do so just to make sure they get the accommodations they want at the next destination. They don't want to be forced to find a different albergue by arriving too late.

It took us a while, but just when we were able to agree on a time to have our morning taxi show up, Dan said something that really got under my skin.

"I don't think I'm going to backtrack with you guys tomorrow. I'm gonna explore Pamplona."

He said it like he didn't give a rip he was choosing to skip walking a part of the Camino. It was as if it didn't matter to him if he walked the whole thing or not.

What. The. Deuce.

That's what went through my head because I had never considered it as an option.

That's probably not the best way to parse out your feelings, but after some thought I perceived that I was having a conflict of ethics. Dan was on his own Camino. He should be able to do the darn thing the way he wanted to. It was I who apparently didn't think he was a "real" pilgrim if he didn't walk the entire way.

What is a real pilgrim?

As the taxi zoomed toward Pamplona, I considered that question. The reality was this: I was also on my own pilgrimage. I should be able to do the Camino the way I felt it should be done. Am I a real pilgrim if I want to explore Pamplona more that retrace our path and walk the whole way? I always believed a real pilgrim walks the entire journey. No shortcuts. No detours. Yet I also wanted to explore Pamplona because I didn't do it the first time with Hannah. Why should I miss out on the opportunity again? I've already walked the entire way once. What does it matter?

I then remembered someone saying, "A pilgrim allows the journey to shape him. He doesn't shape the journey." In other words, a real pilgrim doesn't make plans. He just goes with the flow.

That saying could be useful, if I believed it at all. Historically, pilgrims planned their journeys to work off a penance or lock in an indulgence to earn and prove their love for God. They weren't shaped by the journey. They shaped it and forced their way through it for something more than a pithy saying. They were dedicated to something that had already shaped them, something to which they had given their lives. The Camino was just a step on the way, a big step, but a step nonetheless.

I agree with the historical purpose of the journey, but I also recognize that doing the Camino can shape you as a person because the first Camino shaped me. It left marks on my soul, moments of freedom and failure that shaped my second pilgrimage. I began to understand that my journey wasn't a "one-or-the-other" situation. I shape my Camino and it, in return, shapes me.

I imagine I had a dumbstruck stare on my face because Dan then looked over at me with a smirk and his left eyebrow raised. "It's my Camino," he said. "I'm gonna do it the way I want."

That night, I decided I was going to explore Pamplona as well. I didn't need to backtrack, and if I did, it wouldn't be out of some sort of fear that I wasn't a real pilgrim. I wanted to see Pamplona, and I wasn't going to allow guilt or anything else to drive me away from what I wanted to do.

Dan does what he loves.

Pilgrim Nick was going to do the same.

The next morning, I woke up to the noise of Tabitha, Kelly, and Roshelle getting ready to leave. Dan was still asleep. It was 6:00 a.m., so I just smirked and rolled over. I don't have to get up. I'm gonna stay and explore Pamplona. Sadly, "I don't have to get up" turned into, "Why the heck can't I fall back asleep?" Half an hour later, I was up and getting ready to see the city.

Pamplona is probably best known for "The Running of the Bulls," a summertime festival event where six decidedly nasty fighting bulls are let loose to run through the narrow streets. For some reason, someone back in 1591 thought it would be a good idea to have people run with the bulls rather than from them. Every year, a bunch of lug nuts show their bravado and line the streets for a chance to race alongside (and then jump away from) these stampeding beasts.

I guess everyone has his thing, but that was definitely not mine—and because the bull weren't running, I had no worries about being gored during my exploration.

Ernest Hemingway wrote his novel, The Sun Also Rises, in the Café Iruña, which sits in the town square. That's more of my thing. I like Hemingway. His writing style is simple and direct. My game plan was to grab some tapas at the café and people-watch, but before I went to the square, I wanted to see two other things: the old city walls and the Catedral de Santa Maria la Real.

The old city walls are still largely intact, and you can walk along the top of them for a glimpse of what Pamplona used to be. When under Roman control, Pamplona was a strategic enclave in northern Spain, a huge fortress built to last. As the city grew, some of the walls had to be knocked down to keep up with the expansion. Today, locals pass by the walls without a thought and visitors trample over them. I did my part, trekking across history and reading all of the random informational signs.

I had briefly visited the cathedral during my first Camino but didn't really appreciate it because my feet hurt so bad. I had rushed through looking at the walls, statues, and stained glass, but didn't truly take it all in. It took more than 150 years to build the cathedral, so it featured architectural influences running from the Gothic to the Renaissance. What was really fascinating to me is the dedication people have to places like this. Even though I'm naturally entrepreneurial, I can't imagine committing myself to something that would take 15 years to build, much less 150. The resources, manpower, and money required to make something like that happen is insane. I mean, I get annoyed when my microwave takes longer than a minute to cook my lunch.

I decided to spend some time reading, so I went to a coffee shop, ordered an Americano, and opened my Bible to the book of James. I find it pretty intriguing. James was the half-brother of Jesus but didn't become a believer of His claims to be the Son of God until after the death and resurrection of Christ. What is it like to worship your brother as God? I mean, it makes total sense to me that James wouldn't believe for an instant that his brother was God. If my older brother told me he was God, I'd probably recommend a good shrink who wrote lots of prescriptions. Since James didn't believe until he saw his brother crucified and then encountered Him resurrected from the dead, I figure he must have had some interesting things to say.

I'm also drawn to James because his writing is like Hemingway's: straightforward. He talked about the struggle to follow Jesus and exercise faith in God. We tend to avoid struggle and pain, but James says that it's only through that pain that we grow. It's a lot like a pilgrimage. You journey through the pain of the first few days, and if you make it, you find yourself stronger, your feet calloused, and your mind prepared to take on the physical and emotional toll of the next day.

Or, maybe after the first few days, you find yourself willing to explore Pamplona because you realize not everything hinges on you walking every mile of the pilgrimage. You realize it's not about the steps you take but about the faith that makes you take those steps.

So, I indeed explored Pamplona, walked the old city walls, and read informational signs. I ate tapas at the café and imagined Hemingway smoking and drinking as he wrote his book. I explored the cathedral, took in the paintings and statues, and learned that kings were buried under the floor.

I walked on the graves of kings. How interesting.

What does that even mean?

I'm glad I explored Pamplona—and learned to better appreciate faith along the way.

Isn't that the point? The Camino is a means to foster a deeper or better perspective of faith, life, and relationships, a true "way" to engage with a renewed understanding of self. It pushes you to realize it's not the day-to-day that really matters but your perspective of what happens in the day-to-day that gives each moment its meaning.

6

OVER THE NEXT 28 DAYS OF MY SECOND CAMINO, I LEARNED A LOT about myself, my faith, and why I love the things I do. At first, I spent time asking myself, "What in the world is God going to show me?" For a while, I was expecting another deeply emotional and revealing moment like I had during the first Camino. In fact, I wanted one and found myself frustrated and annoyed that it wasn't happening.

Why can't I connect with God like I did the first time?

The thought charged through my mind like one of those bulls stampeding down the streets of Pamplona, crushing the joy of every step I took. I struggled to cage my discontent, control it, and make sure it couldn't be loosed.

Control your mind.

Focus.

Don't think about it.

Then I flipped the script. No. Think about it a lot. Spend all of your time thinking about it because it's not going away. Search through it and ask the right question. That's what you need to do.

What causes people to have a revelation on the Camino? What caused me to have a moment where I experienced intimacy with God unlike I ever had before?

In Puente de la Reina, I read Ecclesiastes 1:4-7. It said, "A generation goes, and a generation comes, but the earth remains forever. The sun rises, and the sun goes down, and hastens to the place where it rises. The wind blows to the south and goes around to the north; around and around goes the wind, and on its circuits the wind returns. All streams run to the sea, but the sea is not full; to the place where the streams flow, there they flow again."

Ecclesiastes was most likely written by King Solomon, believed to be the wisest and possibly richest guy to ever live. And what does the smartest, wealthiest guy have to say about how the world functions? It runs on a circuit. The sun rises and descends, just to rise and descend again. The wind blows around the globe just to start where it finished.

That is called a liturgy—and recognizing it blew my mind.

I should explain.

Liturgy is an old churchy word most people don't understand. It basically describes the repeated actions and phrases within a religious service. That's not exciting, but the word became interesting for me when I asked myself why churches such as those along the Camino path historically featured "liturgical" practices during their services. For example, when you walk into a Catholic church service, you experience the same things over and over: stand at this phrase, kneel at the other one, now it's time to sit—then repeat.

Turns out liturgy was formed because an old dead guy, or a few old dead guys, realized the world and everyone's daily lives are filled with liturgy without them even knowing it. Think about it. We have routines, things that we naturally do, every day, and those things form what we believe and even what we love. Our hearts naturally long for certain things. We do those things, and we justify why we do them. Yet do we think about these things before we do them? I don't. Most of the time I just do—and it's only when I'm questioned that I begin to wonder why I made the choices I did. My heart desires something. I do it. I justify myself afterward. That's a liturgy, and that repetition changes and forms what I long for and, therefore, what I love. In the end, what the old dead guys realized is that we do what we love, so if they were going to influence change in people, they would need to change what people did so peoples' loves would change in the process.

What do you automatically do every day? What do you naturally think about or talk about? After you first wake up, do you grab your phone and scroll? I do. The first things I read and give thought to shape my day. But why is it that I immediately grab my phone? I've been trained by repeating that action to the point that I now feel lacking and naked if I don't do it. Liturgy has formed me.

Church liturgy is a reaction to the reality that we perform the same things over and over. It needed a voice in the intentional formation of our daily routine to reform the loves of our hearts.

A Camino rips pilgrims out of their daily routine and away from the natural patterns of their lives, thrusting them into a new atmosphere that forces them to develop a new liturgy. When people start out on a pilgrimage, they begin as an infant. They have absolutely no clue what they're doing. All they know is that they're walking to the next place and their primary concerns are basic needs. "Where am I going to go to the bathroom?" "Where do I eat?" "Is there going to be water?" "How do I find a place to sleep?" They're like a babies trying to figure out the strange new world around them. It's only after those first few days that pilgrims begin to form their new daily routine.

Their new liturgy.

During my first Camino with Hannah, I listened to music, podcasts, and sermons while I walked during the day, especially when my muscles ached or I struggled with blisters or sore feet. This time, though, I decided I wanted to walk with no such distractions. I didn't need to provide a soundtrack for my walk because nature already did. Plus, I didn't desire to distract myself from the pain because pain is part of the journey, and something can be learned from it. I wanted those isolated, silent moments to be filled with talking and listening to God. So, I trekked for hours on end with no intrusive diversions. It was just communion with silence, my pain, and with the Father, Son, and Spirit.

What do you do when there's nothing to distract you? What do you think about when there's nothing to push away the deeper things that have been silenced by the busyness of your life?

It was then, when no one was around and all I needed to worry about was putting one foot in front of the other, that I was reminded God doesn't always use big emotional moments or miraculous signs to shape His people. They happen sometimes: Moses and the Red Sea, Elijah and the chariot of fire, Paul and a blinding light. But those weren't the norm. The way God most commonly reveals Himself is through the mundane. Think about Jesus. He was the perfect person and had the perfect relationship with God the Father. What did He do? He formed a liturgy for Himself. When you read through the Gospels, you will see a pattern emerge in His life rhythms. Right before Christ started His public ministry, He went into the wilderness alone and fasted for 40 days. Then, during His public ministry, you see Jesus regularly leave the crowds to go elsewhere to fast and pray. He needed to get away, to be alone with the Father. He needed to remove Himself from the distractions. He needed the silence.

If I want to be like Jesus—if I want to know God better, to better know who I am—I don't need an emotional event or a miracle. I need to be alone with the Father.

I was trying to force God to give me an experience when He was trying to give me a relationship.

How shallow is that? How true is that? Isn't that the trap that we all fall into? In an age when we have the knowledge of the world at our fingertips, we mindlessly scroll through social media looking for something entertaining, demanding it to be there. I'll follow you or like your post if it "engages" me. I want a good experience. If I don't get it, I scroll on until I find it. Is it possible that the liturgy of social media is forming us to be less relational, more isolated, and more selfish? Is the fact that I can scroll past you if you're not engaging teaching me to only engage when my desires are fulfilled? Is it teaching us to only put out what others will "like" about us, promoting ourselves to others instead of being genuine? I think it is, and it translates into how we relate to our spirituality. I can't tell you how many times I've heard someone say, "If God would just do (fill in the blank), then I would believe in Him." Perform for me, God. Do what I want, or I'll scroll past you.

I walked alone with God, and the thoughts that came in the whistling of the wind revealed that I am in the midst of a struggle. My heart longs for two things: experiential and emotional moments with God, but also the recognition that relationships aren't sustained on those. There's got to be more to my relationship with God than temporary moments of entertainment, more than seeking the next thing that will make me feel good. It's about time that I stopped asking God to perform for me and started digging into the mundane, desiring the relationship more than the experience.

I always started my day by walking about five miles before I ducked into a café for a sip of an Americano and some breakfast. It felt good to get some distance under my feet, and those early walks were the times I was alone the most. I tried to hit the road at about 7:00 a.m. when the trail was pretty empty. That gave me time to process what happened the day before. I needed that daily opportunity to get into my own head, to understand what I was thinking and feeling. Back home I tended to get so busy that I really didn't have time to think about what was happening or process what I was feeling. So, those mornings walking alone— thinking, realizing, growing—were some of the most intimate moments between me and the Lord.

Moments where I began to understand the slow, patient love of God and who I am in light of His love. Moments where I realized that I am fully known to Him, even if I didn't fully know myself, and that I have a God who walks with me as I try to search out the depths of my heart.

My liturgy during the Camino became about having no other responsibility but to walk and think.

But every pilgrim has his own liturgy, his own way of processing the journey and dealing with the obstacles. Dave, a semi-retired water aerobics therapist, crossed my path more than a few times. He was a total hippie, doing yoga outside of the albergues, making up songs about other pilgrims and singing them for everyone, and talking about how each of us has our own path to enlightenment. We could not have been more different philosophically, but I genuinely liked him. In his late fifties, Dave was lean with dirty blonde, slightly thinning hair, and he constantly wore a huge smile.

One day we found ourselves sitting outside an albergue, and I asked him about his daily routine here and how it was different from what he did back home. I don't think he had really thought about it much because he was usually quick with a response. Or, maybe he paused because he had been thinking about it and felt his response was important. Either way, when he did answer, he surprised me.

"Back home, I don't really have a schedule. I get up whenever I feel like it. I go shopping sometimes, maybe do a little research, but if I'm not working that day, I don't really have anything to do." As he said it, I noted a tinge of sadness, even longing, in his voice.

"How often do you work?" I asked, seeing that Dave's trademark smile was gone.

"Maybe two or three days a week, and honestly, it's not really engaging or important." He leaned back, sipping his tea. Dave didn't drink alcohol because he believed it wasn't healthy. I had just friggin' walked 18 miles and that was all the healthy I wanted for the moment, so I nursed a whiskey. Straight up, no ice.

"I guess what's been really good for me on the Camino is that I get more exercise than at home," he continued, "and I have structure here. Something to do, to look forward to each morning." His smile was coming back.

"Here, I get to hike every day," Dave said. "I get to meet new people and learn about different cultures. I get to help people when their joints hurt or their tendons are sore. Here, I plan where I'm going and how long it's gonna take."

Kelly overheard him and interrupted to ask if he could check out Roshelle's shins. She had developed shin splints during a particularly difficult day. He apologized to me and then excused himself to attend to Roshelle, excited as could be.

At first, I was slightly annoyed with Kelly for cutting into my time with Dave, but seeing his response to being asked to help reminded me that I needed to chill out.

I'll finish my conversation with him later. Dave needs this. He needs structure. Purpose. Then I thought, I wonder how many people work toward retirement and then find themselves purposeless when they get there.

Roshelle first got shin splints pretty early on in the trek. More than a few pilgrims, including me, suggested loosening her laces. Tying your boots too tight can cause quite a few problems. However, the more I thought about it, the more I realized she probably got shin splints because she was keeping pace with me. Roshelle is in really good shape. She boxes a few times a week, hikes, and does Krav Maga, an Israeli self-defense and fighting style. She could probably whup me in a brawl. Yet my hiking pace was naturally faster than hers, so she likely hurt herself from straining too much to keep up.

By the end of the trip, her body adjusted and she often outpaced me. She got strong and fast, not from training or focusing on it, but because she enjoyed our walking together. I think she really wanted to have an epiphany of her own but was struggling with the fact that it hadn't come.

Back in Tucson, Roshelle is driven, working on the hardest projects and constantly challenging herself. She reminds me of myself. I'm always going, always doing some new, terribly hard thing while exclaiming, "It'll be easy!" It rarely is, of course, but I do it anyway without a second thought, and when I finally do stop and think about it, the answer doesn't take long to surface.

I never feel like I'm good enough. I start new projects, hoping that I will fulfill a need, and then justify why I do them afterward.

I wonder if Roshelle is like me: self-doubting, self-questioning, and looking for validation.

Instead of finding an epiphany during her Camino, Roshelle admitted that she just daydreamed. She said she'd try to listen to the Bible on her iPhone, or think about something she needed to work through, but she always returned to daydreaming.

Why is that a bad thing?

Maybe it was good that she could daydream. What else did she have to do on the Camino? She had no work. She had no projects. She could take a break from solving problems and wonder about, well, anything.

Children daydream. I think they do it because they believe anything can happen, and they feel safe enough to imagine the impossible. They could grow up to be an astronaut. Or a dinosaur. I wanted to be Batman.

Now I just wanted to be like a child.

A few times in the Bible Jesus talks about children. One of the things He mentions more than once is the idea that we need to approach God like children. Specifically, He says something like, "Unless you receive the kingdom of God like a child, you won't enter it." That's the same as saying, "If you want to become a Christian, you have to be like a kid." That's a pretty big deal, so a lot of people then wonder, "How does a kid view God?"

God is loving. God is kind. God is the strongest and can do anything.

But I think most people make the mistake of focusing on God rather than on the kid. "How do I enter the kingdom of God like a child?"

What does a child naturally assume about others?

"You want me."

Kids have the audacity to assume everyone wants them around and wants good for them. That's why we have to teach them concepts such as "stranger danger." They simply trust that everyone loves them. Those kids being brought to Jesus in the Bible automatically assumed Christ wanted to bless them.

Yet we tend to approach God differently. We ask, "Does God really want me?" "Does He really love me?" "Honestly, just as I am with all the mistakes and all the messes that exist in my life?"

I wonder if anyone really believes God wants them around and loves them just as they are?

Probably not.

In fact, I imagine they believe that if they are gonna get in good with God they need to fix a past problem first. Over and over I hear, "I'll follow Jesus after I clean up my life." That's what they say instead of simply coming to Him, assuming, "You obviously love me. Why wouldn't you? I'm me!"

One of the most common perceptions I've come across as a pastor is that people view God the same way they view their own father. I mean, it makes sense. As a kid, your dad is basically a demi-god. He can pick you up and whirl you around without any effort. He's the smartest and can fix anything. Your mom is soft and gentle, but your dad, he has calloused hands and a scruffy face. He's hairy and a little smelly. His voice is deeper and he's a little scary.

Dad is God.

As a father, the idea that my children may see me that way is terrifying. Bad dads leave more damage than they realize. Everyone thinks kids are resilient—that they'll recover from the messy divorce, forget about their father's anger issues, look the other way about his drunkenness, or gloss over the fact that their father was never around. Kids seem to be resilient because to them, no matter what, their dad is still the best. It's not until they get older or have a new father figure step into their lives that they begin to realize, "Dad messed up."

Kids are quick to recover and bounce back until they actually recognize what they've been through, realize how it has shaped and formed their current lives, and begin to assess how it has caused them to have problems in their lives and defects in their relationships with others.

I met more than a few pilgrims who had some interesting things to say about their dads. Quite a few had abusive fathers, whether that was physical, emotional, or mental, and they all came out of it with a negative view of God. They saw an angry and distant God, one that they would never be good enough for. One who really didn't care about them.

One man I talked with during the Camino had a father who got drunk and physically abused his mom. He explained to me how he was never big enough to stop his father when he was a kid but remembered being so happy when his parents divorced. He started the Camino after me but walked two-thirds of it hustling upwards of 40 kilometers a day. When we met, he was slowing his pace due to an injury and told me stories of graduating at the top of his class, taking care of his family, and starting businesses. Essentially, this guy succeeded at everything he did. He became powerful, maybe even powerful enough to stop a drunk dad, so he explained that he didn't need God and, therefore, didn't believe in Him.

On the other hand, I met a chef near the end of my pilgrimage who also didn't believe in a god at all but admitted, "If I did, I would believe in my father's god. My father is a good man and loves his family well."

Good dads can give their children an idea of the wonder of who God is. Good dads can make their children want to believe.

Being a demi-god is a big deal, and for me, the fact that I share the name "father" with God, my heavenly Father, makes that weight even bigger. Yet I have this crazy belief that God has it all under control, meant for me to have my specific children, and that no matter what, with all my faults and failures, I am the best dad for them. I trust that God is going to draw my kids to Himself. He's going to show them who He really is, and He's going to use me in that process. When all is said and done, I hope my kids will have the childlike audacity to assume, "God wants me."

7

EVERY PILGRIM I KNOW HAS HAD THAT "ONE DAY." IT'S THE DAY THAT makes you want to quit, the day that pummels you until you wonder why you ever even wanted to walk this freakin' trail to begin with.

That day came for me traveling from Hontanas to Boadilla del Camino. It's an 18-mile trek across rolling hills and wheat fields, a terrain and distance generally in my comfort zone. I usually started a walk that distance by hitting the trail no later than 7:00 a.m. so I could walk it at a relaxed pace and finish around 2:00 p.m., giving me the rest of the day to read, hang out, and talk with other pilgrims.

I loved 18-mile days. I just hated the journey from Hontanas to Boadilla del Camino.

I woke up later than usual that morning, leaving me a little stressed as I worked to get my gear in order and get out the door. It was pouring pretty hard, too, so I needed to put on my jacket which, as I've already shared, I hate doing when I hike. I decided that the morning was going to be a wash because the air was chilly and the sky overcast, but surely the day would get better once the sun came out. No big deal.

The morning actually turned out to be pretty great, and I had the weather to thank for it. You see, I love watching people slip and fall. Does that mean I'm a bad person? Probably. Maybe it just suggests I need a good therapist. Either way, the trails were super slick with mud, and the mire sent pilgrims sliding wherever the path turned downhill. The group I was in, which included Roshelle, Kelly, Dan, and a few new friends, traveled in a straight line at one point because the trail was so narrow, and more than a few times I watched from behind as someone made that funny jerky movement they do when their feet start to slide out from underneath them. Their arms flailed up into the air as they grasped for something, anything, to balance them (usually the pilgrim behind or in front of them), and that would cause the second pilgrim to slip and do the same thing. People couldn't help but laugh, and I probably laughed most of all. We must've looked like a column of drunk ducks waddling our way through the muck, which made me laugh even more.

By 11:00 a.m., our wobbly line pulled into a little café to warm up, dry off, and get something to eat. The place was quaint with a nice fireplace in the corner opposite the bar where we placed our orders. I decided to get an orange juice after watching the barkeep meticulously cut and squeeze the citrus for someone else. I love orange juice about as much as I love watching fail videos on YouTube. I don't know if I have a Vitamin C deficiency or something, but I can drink an entire quart of the stuff in one sitting. Hannah constantly warns me not to drink too much because I always feel sick afterward, but it's to no avail. I am basically a 180-pound toddler with no self-control.

After warming up, we all headed out again, and by the time we made it through the town, the rain had stopped but the wind had kicked up to almost a gale. It was so strong that it forced me to either walk at an angle or be blown to the other side of the trail. It was so loud that I couldn't hear a thing except its incessant roaring in my ears. I may hate walking in the rain, but I soon confirmed that I hated walking in the wind even more.

Outside of the town was a nice patch of prairie for a couple of miles before the path shot straight up the side of a giant hill that seemed much more like a small mountain. Whatever its topographical classification, I remembered it from the first Camino and recalled it was not an easy ascent before it plateaued for 100 yards and then dropped steeply down the other side.

As I made my way toward it, my thoughts grew grim. This is gonna suck, especially with all this wind! By the time I hit the base of the thing I had totally psyched myself out. I was sure that all I was going to do was struggle and slog. I had already lost the battle before it started.

Your mindset really does make or destroy any journey you make or obstacle you face. I had hiked countless hills and mountains far more difficult than that one, but I chose to approach it negatively—and that ruined my day.

Deciding it was best just to hustle up and over, I pressed hard against the wind and leaned toward the mountain, taking sure, hard steps. My left knee started getting sore, but I didn't want to lose my momentum, so I didn't stop to put on my brace. Halfway up, the wind blew off my hat and sent it barreling down the trail and then off the side.

> Dear Wind,
>
> I hate you. I hate everything about you. I even hate your mom, if you have a mom. If you do, she probably hates you, too. I hope you die.
>
> Sincerely,
> Nicholas H. Lang

As I turned to chase after my hat, Roshelle passed me with a cherubic smile on her face that indicated she was somehow enjoying this. The thing is, I knew she was enjoying it because she loved the challenge, and that frustrated me to no end. I just couldn't shake my crappy, defeated attitude. My left knee really started to scream at me as I dropped down the trail to get my hat. Going downhill destroys knees, especially bad ones, but I was so frustrated and annoyed that I pushed through it.

I found my hat snagged in a thorn bush about 15 feet off the trail. Problem was, I didn't realize it was a thorn bush until I was waist deep in it, and every one of those little boogers was piercing my skin. I grabbed my hat and tried to exit my pointy prison as quickly and painlessly as possible, but I could feel the thorns ripping little holes in my pants and slashing my skin.

I hate the rain, I hate the wind, and I hate thorn bushes.

When I finally reached the plateau, I dropped my pack and pulled off my jacket to try to enjoy the view, but I just couldn't manage it. I didn't realize how much I had been sweating, and as soon as I took my jacket off, the wind hit my shirt, and I started shivering. The views were beautiful, but I didn't give a rip. At that point, I just wanted off that stupid hill. So, I headed down the other side.

What is the point of this mountain? I groused inwardly. Nothing. There is no point. You are useless.

My knee sent shock waves of pain through my body with every step. I figured that once I got to the bottom, I could slap on my brace and it would all be fine. But when I got there, the pain was so bad that I had to sit down for a while and massage it. As I did, I realized the damage was done. Every step was going to hurt the rest of the way, even with the brace.

I walked the rest of the day angry at myself because I hadn't put on the brace when I first thought about it. Every step reminded me that I had ruined the day for myself, and that my mindset had been so negative that I turned something challenging into something that destroyed my journey. I walked in sulking silence, frustrated and mad as I was buffeted by the wind.

When I finally reached the albergue, Roshelle was there eating some snacks. When she saw me, she exclaimed, "I really liked the hike today."

Mindset is everything.

We all have our mountains. Whether or not we cross them, and how we feel during the process, is not based on the mountain itself but on how we approach it, how we view it, and how we traverse it.

A lot of stories in the Bible come to mind when I think about how I decide to approach obstacles—especially mountains—in my life. Scripture is full of people doing radically insane things, and one of my favorites is Abraham. In Genesis 12, Abraham (then called Abram) heard a voice that told him to go to a land that "the voice" would show him, and he simply does it. He leaves his father, mother, and siblings, packs up his belongings, grabs his wife, and says, "We're gonna go follow that voice. It's the true voice."

If I'm his dad, I'm thinking, "Man, I knew that bump to the head as a kid did some damage."

But Abraham followed the voice and left on an insane journey to do an absolutely insane thing, and the voice, God, made him the father of nations. Abraham embarked on the journey not just believing in himself, but in something greater, trusting that Someone was showing him the way. His mountain, though, didn't come until decades later after he and his wife, Sarah, had Isaac, the promised son the voice said would be born even though Abraham and Sarah were way too old to have kids.

In Genesis 22, God told Abraham to do a very strange thing. The Lord instructed him to take his only son, the promised son, on a hike up a mountain—to sacrifice him. That is, go to the summit, build an altar made of large stones, put some kindling and logs on top, tell Isaac to lay down on them, and then slit his throat.

It's a grisly story to say the least and leaves a really bad taste in the mouths of a lot of people who read it. They wonder, "How can God, if there is such a thing, ask a man to sacrifice his own son just to appease Him? How can that God be considered loving, generous, or even wanting what is good for mankind?"

I get that. But the bigger question for me is, "How could Abraham do it?"

I mean, he got up early in the morning and took his son, who is now most likely around 37 years old, and trekked him up the mountain. He even had Isaac carry the wood that he was going to burn on, which logically prompted Isaac to ask, "Where is the lamb for the a sacrifice?" Now remember, Abraham was old, "Guinness Book of World Records" old, and Isaac was a man, not some guy-that-lives-with-his-mom-and-plays-video-games-in-the-basement sort of man, but one who labored in the field, herding cattle, hauling hay, and digging post holes. Isaac had calluses, a good ol' boy tan line, and could probably hurl me about 30 yards if I tried to steal one of his sheep.

Don't mess with Isaac.

Yet Abraham simply replied, "God will provide for himself the lamb for a burnt offering, my son." The words ring off the page as if Abraham didn't have a care in the world, like he completely believed what he was saying even before the words left his lips.

"Yeah. God's got this."

To everyone's astonishment, big, burly Isaac just went along with it. He didn't ask any questions, push back, or push his crazy Pops over the nearest ledge. He obediently carried the logs to his demise. At least, that's what the story leaves us to assume, but I think that there is way more to the tale. You see, Isaac knew his dad. He knew his father had been following the voice of God for a long time, and he also knew that he was the promised son. I believe Isaac realized his father would climb any mountain and do anything God told him to do, no matter how crazy it was.

Most of all, Isaac knew you don't climb a mountain to sacrifice an animal to God if you don't have an animal to begin with. There's no chance he didn't realize that he was the sacrifice. Isaac walked on, though, climbing the mountain and carrying his burden of wood through the pain and frustration. He ascended to the peak with his father at his side—the man who was going to perform the sacrifice.

Most good stories end there, at the peak, the top, the ultimate destination where dreams are fulfilled and the sacrifices feel justified— but not for these two. For Abraham and Isaac, the peak is where the sacrifice is going to happen, where what they actually believe is going to be revealed, and where they will discover if they have the grit to follow through with what they've decided to do. With what they've been told to do.

Here three stories intersect: the accounts of Abraham, Isaac, and God. Abraham was to build the altar that God commanded him to construct, but he wasn't going to do it alone. Isaac, the younger and stronger of the two, was going to do the heavy lifting, supporting his father and ensuring Abraham was still the "man" even though he was up in years. Abraham then "bound Isaac his son and laid him on the altar ... reached out his hand and took the knife to slaughter his son." (Genesis 22:9-10)

Incredible! At this point, did Abraham believe in himself or God? Was he relying on his belief that he'd follow through, no matter the cost, to obey the voice that he had heard, the voice that had been so faithful to him? The voice that used to be gentle but was now severe? Or was Abraham relying on nothing more than his own grit?

We don't know, but I'm inclined to think he already knew what he was capable of doing. I believe Abraham knew he was going to get up early that morning and hike his son up that mountain fully prepared to do whatever God asked him to do. I also think Abraham truly believed what he told Isaac when he said God would provide the lamb for the sacrifice. Abraham walked boldly up those trails, and every rock he and his son laid was placed without a tinge of doubt that God was going to come through.

In the end, that's exactly what happened. "The angel of the Lord called to him from heaven and said, 'Abraham, Abraham!' And he said, 'Here I am.' He said, 'Do not lay your hand on the boy or do anything to him, for now I know that you fear God, seeing you have not withheld your son, your only son, from me.'" (Genesis 22:11-12) Then God placed a ram in the thicket nearby, and Abraham's belief, not just in himself but in the transcendent God, proved to be justified.

As Abraham crested the ridge of the mountain, he found that belief in his ability, while good, was not enough. He needed to trust beyond himself.

Then there's Isaac. His dad loved him. He was the heir to everything his father built and was continuing to build. He was the son who heard the stories of "the voice" and learned that it was God. He tended his father's flocks and worked hard for him, not just out of duty but out of love and deep trust. Isaac had surely walked with Abraham in the cool morning, just like Adam did with God—but the walk up that mountain with his father was like none he'd experienced.

When Isaac's mind turned to the practical realities of what they were doing, going to a sacrifice without an animal to offer, his father revealed what God had said about providing the sacrifice for Himself. Isaac continued on, and by the time the climactic moment arrived, he had made the decision to allow his body to be laid out on the altar. He could have wriggled free, pushed his father back, and fled. But he didn't. He made his choice.

Isaac had what it took to get up the mountain. He had the strength to build the altar. He willed his way through being placed on top of it. But the question was, whom did Isaac trust? If he believed in himself, getting to the summit of the mountain would've been enough. If he believed in his father, building the altar would've been enough. Yet I think he, too, believed in something more. Isaac trusted in the God his father believed in. He knew God was going to provide for Himself a sacrifice, which was why he allowed himself to be stretched across the logs with a knife poised above his throat. Isaac realized that believing in himself and his father alone were not enough.

Every mountain is a challenge and the hope of every mountain is that you'll find your happy ending at the peak as long as you believe in yourself. The truth is, that every mountain has an altar calling you to recognize something more that you've always known. Therefore, it's more than mindset alone. It's more than your capability or the strength you can find in yourself. At the top of the mountain, at the very point of sacrifice, you'll discover your need for something bigger than yourself.

You'll need to hear and obey "the voice" to provide for you.

As Roshelle leaned back, eating her snacks and relishing in the good hike she had that day, I looked to the sky and beyond the storm to realize that maybe more than my mindset toward the mountain was off.

Walking through the Meseta on the Camino de Santiago is no small task. A large and expansive flat plain of central Spain, it is by far the most boring part of the month-long journey. The trail has no mountains to defeat and virtually no trees, so the sun relentlessly presses down on you like an overbearing mother. It's mostly farmland, and you find yourself treading forward as you stare at the tiny speck in the distance that is the next town you're desperately trying to get to. However, that speck fosters frustration as you slowly trudge along with nothing to distract or interest you. It infuriates you, and ultimately makes you hopeless because you start to feel like you're never going to make it.

The Meseta brings out different reactions from pilgrims. Some choose to skip the darn thing and grab a taxi through it. Others decide they'll bike across it and knock it out in no time. And there are more than a few who attempt to walk it but give up and quit the Camino altogether. Those who do decide to stick it out usually keep themselves entertained with music or a podcast. Such distractions can take the weight of the Meseta off their shoulders and make it seem like they're getting to the next speck on the horizon a little faster.

But I had determined not to allow myself to be distracted. I was intent on walking the barren land with nothing but my thoughts to keep me company. Of course, being left only to your thoughts can be a dangerous thing because it's then you begin to realize things about yourself that you have subconsciously or purposefully kept from surfacing.

During the Meseta, I quickly accepted that I was bored. Really bored. Not with the walking, per se, but with a lot of the interactions I was having with the other pilgrims I was meeting along the trail.

The conversations were all the same. I'd introduce myself, and they'd introduce themselves. I'd ask where they're from, and then they'd ask me. Then we'd try to make small talk by asking each other about our home countries, where each of us were headed for the day, what we both did for a living, blah blah blah.

Boring.

If I am completely honest, I really don't care where they started or where they're from. I can know those things and still have no clue who the heck I'm walking with. I can know your name and have absolutely no clue about who you really are.

Most people equate much of their identity with what they do for a living, but that alone doesn't encapsulate who someone is—unless they are a workaholic. Even then, though, it's incomplete. Knowing a name, a country, or a profession doesn't really reveal a lot about anyone, and I was tired of the small talk.

So, as I marched across the Meseta, I discovered that if I really wanted to know who a person was, I needed to know more. What do they give themselves to? What are they passionate about? What couldn't they live without? I decided I needed to know what they loved to know who they really are—and that's not boring at all.

"What do you love?"

Now that's a question, huh? It's intimate, revealing, and will tell you a whole lot more about yourself than anything else; if, that is, you're completely honest with yourself. After all, it's also a dangerous question, maybe one you're not quite ready to answer. You might even push it away.

From then on, I resolved that was going to be the question I asked others, even if it did push them away. I mean, why should I expect anyone to actually answer it in the first place?

On a road between two wheat fields that looked like they had just been harvested, I came across Chef. He was pale, not in a sickly sort of way, but a guy who obviously got sunburned if he even thought about getting a tan. He looked like he was in his late twenties and trekked at a good pace, but he wore knee and ankle braces on his right leg. I had been walking alongside Bridget earlier, but she had gotten caught up in a conversation with a girl from New Zealand and they were moving pretty slowly, so I decided to let them be, and I eventually caught up to Chef.

I matched his pace, and we both walked silently together for a while. Well, that's not entirely true. You can't walk silently with anyone. Shoes crunch on the ground, clothes shift and rub as you move, the staff thuds as it hits the ground, stuff like that. There's so much noise, but nothing is as loud as the dialogue going on in your head. That's what makes walking in "silence" next to someone you don't know so tricky. Should I break the silence? Do they want me to break the silence? What if I sound like an idiot? What if they're annoying?

I finally got up the nerve and introduced myself—and after we began the blah blah blah pilgrim ritual, I jumped right in with both feet. "What do you love, Chef?"

He was quiet for a few seconds and then pressed, "Why do you ask?"

I explained to him my thoughts on the conversations that pilgrims have and began to ramble on about how I didn't think you can really get to know someone until you know what they love. Chef seemed to be listening, so I decided to ask again.

"I'm not sure," he responded, looking at the road in front of him. "I don't think I've ever really thought about it."

I decided to give him a little help by telling him about some of the things I love, ranging from God and family to business and cooking. I talked about missing my wife and kids and how I think I have the best church in the world. I shared how I really love the freedom I experience when I hike. I hoped to inspire him to think of something he loved.

Instead, he just said, "You love a lot of things."

"Well, I've thought about this for a while," I replied, trying to sound lighthearted because it was definitely becoming a very awkward conversation.

Chef continued staring at the ground and walking in silence. The background noisiness returned, and I concluded I'd just stop talking.

Well, that sucks, I thought to myself, You definitely just made him feel uncomfortable instead of getting to know him. Now you're THAT guy, the weirdo who asks prying questions.

Fifteen minutes later, Chef started to slow down. I could tell he was favoring his bad leg and figured he was going to stop, at which point I'd offer to carry his pack for a while in an attempt to reengage. When he did stop, though, he didn't complain about his leg at all, but instead pulled out a big ol' bottle of sunscreen and began to slather it all over his face, arms, and legs. It was the perfect time for me to retry and break us out of our quiet coexistence.

"Hey, man. Do you wanna transfer some of your stuff into my pack? Yours looks pretty heavy."

"Nah, I'm good," he said, bending over to sunscreen his good leg.

"What happened to your knee?" I queried carefully.

"I broke my ankle earlier this year, and it's been pretty sore. I think walking with a bad ankle did something to my knee."

"Dude, that sucks," I said. "Are you sure you don't want help with the pack?" I already knew the answer was going to be "no."

"No worries. I've carried it this far," he responded as he put his sunscreen back in his pack and began to walk again. He started looking at the ground once more, and I figured I'd just match his pace.

Then he looked up and said, "My mom."

"What do you mean?" I asked, caught off guard.

"I think I love my mom." His voice was a little shaky, and it almost sounded like he was a little embarrassed by what he had just revealed.

"Dude, you've gotta tell me about your mom."

Chef and I walked together almost every day for the rest of the Camino. If we weren't walking together, we stayed in the same town. When we were with people, Chef was quick-witted and sarcastic, a lot like Kelly. But the days that we walked on the trails just the two of us, he was ready to talk about the deeper things, the harder things. As I learned more about him and his life, I realized he had overcome some ridiculous odds. The cards had been stacked against him and he could have let them crush him, but he didn't. Chef started out surrounded by abuse and addiction, but he made himself into an extremely successful entrepreneur who owned a chain of restaurants. He was determined—determined enough to carry that huge pack for 500 miles with a bad leg. More than that, he was smart. He used his grit and his brains and pulled himself out of a life that offered only pain and struggle to make something of himself.

It was a good story.

It wasn't a great one, though. Chef dragged himself out of poverty, but he still couldn't think of anyone or anything that he truly loved. Even when he did mention his mother, it was still with some doubt. He spent so much time fighting against the things holding him down and straining toward his goals that he forgot how to love. In the end, Chef was walking the Camino because he was trying to figure out whether or not he was going to leave the empire he had built. He had achieved his dreams but had begun to hate them because they left him feeling empty.

So, he decided to walk and think. Hopefully, I helped him somehow along the way.

Chef taught me something really important: determination, wits, and achievements are good. They'll leave you with a good story. Without love, though, it'll never be a great one.

Love is king.

Love may be king, but it's also complicated—really complicated. Kings are fickle and kingdoms are hard to rule. I learned that from Laura, whom I came across often enough for her to tell me her life story. I got my chance to ask her what she loved in Mansilla de las Mulas. I made good time that day and arrived in town earlier than expected, so I locked down a bed in one of the albergues and decided to visit the bar across the street to have a scotch.

I drink scotch "neat" in case you're wondering. If you want to know why (or maybe learn what "neat" is), you can take me out for one and ask.

After an hour or so, I had decided to sit outside the bar at one of their little red plastic tables to sip my scotch, read my Bible, and smoke a cigarette when Laura walked up and plopped down in one of the chairs.

"Whew, it's good to see you!" she declared as she picked up a menu and began looking through it. "I got completely lost walking through town, and when I saw you, I knew I was headed in the right direction."

Some of the towns along the Camino can be confusing because the signs leading the way fade or get covered up. I told her it was good to see her, too, but my mind was wandering because I had just finished reading the book of Ecclesiastes, which essentially says that all of life is meaningless apart from living for and loving God.

That's heavy.

Feeling contemplative, I decided to ask her what she loved, and her initial response was more like Chef's than I expected. She went quiet for a few seconds.

"That's a hard question," she admitted, genuine but obviously struggling to come up with an answer.

"Well, let's flip it over. Who do you struggle to love?" I figured the answer would be simple: Democrats, Republicans, the religious, the judgmental, or something like that.

Then Laura surprised me.

"Myself." She said it quickly, looking me in the eye, without a doubt. She had been thinking about this, I thought to myself. "Why?"

"I don't know." She sighed heavily. "I really don't know, but I struggle loving people who have expectations of me, too."

Laura didn't realize it, but her reply made a whole lot of sense to me. She'd grown up in a home with two parents. Two parents who failed her. Her dad flew off the handle at any given moment and beat her, especially if she did something wrong. Sometimes he used a belt, sometimes his hands, and sometimes he choked her. She had already told me one horror story after another about the chaos she lived in as a little girl.

I'm a pacifist, but if I wasn't—well, let's just be glad I am.

Laura's mother wasn't aggressive. She just caved, allowing it all to happen. There's no doubt in my mind she was abused, too. But with no obvious evidence, Laura was left in a precarious situation. What do you do when your dad assaults you? What do you feel when your mom doesn't stand up for you?

The biggest question, though, was what did all that say about who Laura was? I think the answer for her was unlovable. She had a hard time loving herself because the two people who were supposed to love her didn't show it or make her feel worthy of love. It made me wonder who caused the most damage in Laura's life. Which parent was more culpable for Laura's inability to love herself: the aggressor or the one who stood by and did nothing while it was happening?

I didn't know, but I did discover that there was hope for Laura. Sitting there outside the bar, she then told me she was an event coordinator back home in New Zealand before she quit her job to wander through Spain. One of her last gigs, she told me, was for a church. She then revealed she was not religious—and when I say, "not religious," I mean she was anti-God. Not only anti-God, she was anti-anyone who believed in God. "When I found out you were a pastor the second day we walked together," she said, "it blew me away that I didn't hate you."

Anyway, anti-God Laura said she was coordinating an event for this church, some sort of conference or something, and at the end of it all the religious people, whom she really disliked, decided to take communion together. Communion made her feel uncomfortable. "It's this weird ritual where people pretend to eat Jesus. Why would you pretend to eat another human being?" she asked. "I didn't want anything to do with it." So, she told me she slipped into a side room to wait until communion was finished and she could organize the clean-up.

At least that was her plan.

Instead, she said the pastor of the group came into the room and invited her to take communion with them. "Oh, I'm not a Christian or religious or anything," she told him, trying to worm her way out of it.

"Well, we just want you to feel loved and included," the pastor replied. "You worked really hard on organizing this."

"Thanks," she said, surprised by the unexpected compliment, "but isn't it against the rules?" Laura asked. "Since I don't believe in God?"

She said the pastor then told her something she was not at all anticipating. "I think God cares more about you being included and loved than He does about rules."

I like that pastor. I'd buy him a scotch any day.

When Laura finished telling me that story, she had a slight quiver in her voice. It was as though she could picture the room and the pastor, as if it was still happening as she spoke.

"I'd never been so shocked but felt so cared for at the same time," she told me. "I mean, I don't even believe the same thing as they do, but they still invited me in to do this super holy religious thing with them. Who does that?"

"Jesus does. He loves people right where they're at." I'd said it without thinking because I was engulfed in the story and tend to speak without thinking anyway. When I heard the words leave my mouth, I immediately got nervous. I had no clue how she was going to react or if I came off way too religious.

Crap, man. You probably just ruined this really good moment!

I didn't, though. Instead of an awkward silence, she looked up and said, "He might love me. If I believed in him." Then a big smile came across her face. "I can't believe I just told that to a pastor! I haven't told that to anyone, not even my girlfriend."

Laura ended up getting shin splints a few days after our conversation outside the bar, and I lost track of her. But I can't stop thinking of that smile she gave me, realizing she could share something so intimate with me, someone she normally would have hated. I'm honored she did, but I'm even happier she experienced love and acceptance as an outsider from that pastor.

She got to know what it was like to have someone act with love toward her rather than have someone who was supposed to love her hurt her instead.

Yes. There's hope for Laura.

While walking to Rabanal del Camino, I was thinking ahead to the Cruz de Ferro. That's the iron cross atop a five-meter wooden pole where, during the first Camino, Hannah and I each placed a rock to symbolize leaving our burdens behind at the feet of Jesus. It's a significant stop for many pilgrims along the Camino de Santiago—and I knew that the next day I was going to be standing on the top of that mountain staring at the cross ready to leave something beneath it.

I hadn't planned to leave anything there this time around, but before I left Tucson, Hannah slipped a letter into my pack when I wasn't looking. When I found the letter on the first day of the Camino, I read it three or four times. I could hear her voice and feel her love as she encouraged me on my journey. Hannah was the one who really wanted me to do another pilgrimage, and she sacrificed so that I could. Reading that note reminded me about how much I am loved and supported.

At least it did in the beginning.

Now, only one day away from the Cruz de Ferro, the letter felt like a 500-pound weight. As I'd read it every day before, it was reminding me about how much I missed my wife and kids, Rosie and Clara. That transitioned really quickly into making me feel guilty for even thinking about the Camino, much less doing it a second time. Most days when I began feeling guilty, I told myself I was doing what Hannah wanted for me. Every time I had talked myself out of the trip, she talked me right back into it.

"You need this, babe," she'd say, "and I want you to have it."

The morning I left for Rabanal and read the letter again, the paper was starting to get so worn from folding and unfolding it that it was starting to fall apart and fade—and that's when it hit me. The paper was neon green—and came from the same batch of neon green paper that I had bought for the kids not long before I left. We got it, along with other bright shades of paper, so that Rosie and Clara could have an activity to look forward to every day while I was away. I had cut the bright sheets into thin slits, then wrote a note and drew a picture on each one, 35 in all. I made a chain of each of those notes so Hannah and the kids could undo a link and read it each night.

Suddenly, I could picture Rosie and Clara reading the little notes and playing with them. I could hear their giggles and squeals during story time at night, and I could see their smiles as Hannah wrangled them into their PJs. I started thinking about how much I missed my family.

You can miss someone so much that it physically hurts. In your bones.

I also started to think about how difficult it must be for Hannah, trying to play both our roles while I was gone. The night before I had talked with her on the phone, and she was exhausted and frustrated, and one of the girls was crying and throwing a fit in the background. She had to cut our conversation short because she was having such a hard time.

All at once, I felt like a crappy husband and dad because I basically abandoned them for a month to take a long walk. What kind of husband

and father leaves his family for a month to wander through Spain? I brooded. Probably not a good one.

As I approached Rabanal, I simply couldn't shake the guilt I was feeling. Distracting myself wasn't working. Reminding myself of what Hannah had told me was useless, and I descended deeper and deeper into unrelenting self-blame. I wanted to quit. I wanted to stop, hail a taxi, get to the nearest airport, and go home with my tail tucked between my legs and repent for being a terrible husband and father.

Yet I also knew I wouldn't quit because even though emotionally I was feeling like a dirt bag, intellectually I knew that every step of the Camino was a gift from my wife to me—and you don't throw away a gift like that, one born out love and sacrifice.

So, what do you do when you feel guilty? Get rid of the thing that causes it. I decided I was going to leave the letter at the foot of the Cruz de Ferro. I told myself it was going to symbolize and honor the sacrifice Hannah made for me and the struggle she was having back home. It was heroic, a gesture of love. Plus, I was going to honor my children and how much I loved them.

I was going to leave the letter there—well, honestly, because I was lying to myself. The truth was I was tired of reading it and feeling guilty. I no longer wanted to feel like a failure, and I needed to shed that weight. Fast.

The next morning, I got up and stepped on the trail ready and determined to drop the weight of my guilt at the Cruz de Ferro. Of course, that morning brought terrible hiking conditions. The sky was dropping buckets of rain on me, so much that my jacket couldn't keep me dry, and then the wind picked up. It began blowing so hard that it made the rain hitting my face feel like a million little icy needles.

I hate the wind, I hate the rain, and I hated the weight of the letter.

Three miles into the trek, I came to a small town and decided to duck into one of the cafes. I was wet, annoyed, and ready to quit hiking for the day. What I knew I needed right then was a strong Americano and some time to sit and read my Bible.

The Bible, for me, is more than a religious document or a historical narrative. It's good news. It's an explanation of why there's pain and what's being done about it. It expands my view of life from my personal experience to an eternal worldview, and it reveals that all of life, all of my experiences, and everything I do actually has meaning.

The problem with the Bible, though, is the apex of the story, Jesus on the cross. Now, I don't have a problem with Jesus existing or God taking on humanity. Textual translations don't bother me, and neither do miracles. What I do have a problem with is Christ's claim that He takes my guilt and replaces it with grace and salvation as a gift. People seem to be bothered by the fact that not everyone gets to go to heaven. What bothers me is that anyone gets to go at all.

Think about it. God looks at humanity and sees what we are doing to one another and to the earth, and He says, "Hey, I should invite them here, into perfection. They'll do great!" If I were God, not a single soul would make it. People are selfish, arrogant, and violent. If we were honest with ourselves, we'd all admit, "I have some serious defects." But most of the time we're not honest with ourselves, preferring instead to live blindly to our darkest issues.

Then comes Jesus, flying in like Mighty Mouse, here to save the day! He looks at me with powerful, loving eyes and tells me He's gonna save me from my guilt—and not just mine, but everyone else's, even if I don't think they deserve it. I'm a pastor. People tell me things, unspeakable things. Things they've done and things that have happened to them. I hear what's done in the shadows, and I know what people are capable of. Look at history. Look at what mankind does to one another, what we still do to one another! Why would God want to save anyone?

Honestly, I don't think anyone deserves to go to heaven because heaven is perfect, and we'll wreck it. Well, maybe Mother Teresa. She seemed nice enough, but the rest of us are screwed. So, when Jesus comes and says, "I'll take all the weight, all the guilt, myself. I'll drink up all of the wrath due because of your guilt, and I'll give you life and freedom as a gift." That's mind boggling. That is a gift you don't throw away, a gift I'm not sure I could ever offer—

but one I won't let pass by.

The Bible is the story of a gift given to people who don't deserve it.

And then, sitting in that café with my Americano, I knew why Hannah's letter bothered me. I didn't deserve it or her gift of the Camino. But Hannah loves Jesus and tries to be like Him, so she gave me a gift I don't deserve. She gave me something purely out of love, and it was a sacrifice—a sacrifice for her husband who has some serious defects. I realized Hannah's letter, like the Bible, is good news. It's tells me that even though I am not perfect and at times pretty terrible, I am loved, deeply and honestly loved.

I closed my Bible and marched up that hill, through the rain and through the wind, to the Cruz de Ferro with a purpose. I hustled up that mountain quick and strong because I needed to leave something at that cross. When I finally made it, the wind and rain had succumbed to a misty fog that seemed to roll across the mountain like a soothing wave of grace.

I stood at the cross, bent down, and put the letter in my backpack. In its place, I left the guilt, all 500 pounds of it, placing it symbolically, and I believe quite literally, at the feet of my Jesus. The One whose free gift of grace for guilt bothers me so much.

I'm so glad I kept that letter. It's a reminder of the sacrificial love that has been given to me. Allow me to share it with you.

My Husband,

I am so excited for your adventure! The Camino was the first place I've ever really seen you come alive. The fact that you will get that again makes my heart so happy! I always want to love and support you in all your goals, dreams, hopes. Even though I'm not by your side this time around, I am rooting you on every step of the way. Can't wait to hear and see what God does in these 35 days ahead of you. My love, thank you for showing our girls and me what it means to love in action and deed. You are the most selfless person I know. Take in every moment of this trip, be present to what's happening around you—know we will be totally fine! Please, please, please be safe and LISTEN to your body!! You don't have anything to prove because you are loved fully as you are. Come home quick. I love you more than all the steps you will take and all the "Buen Caminos" you will hear!

You've got my heart,
Hannah

Many albergues and restaurants on the Camino offer something called "The Pilgrim Menu." The first course allows you to choose among different types of salad or a soup. For the second course you select chicken, pork, fish, or sometimes a super thin steak that reminds me of what I buy to make carne asada. The final course is the dessert: ice cream, flan, or yogurt. The Pilgrim Menu only costs 10 euros, a steal because it comes with wine and bread. The only problem is the food is bland. I'm pretty sure the cook is allergic to seasoning. I hate paying for food I know I can cook better.

Early in each Camino, the flavorless food really didn't bother me. By the time dinner rolled around, I was starving and scarfed it down so fast I couldn't taste it anyway. However, once my body got used to all the exercise, I slowed down and enjoyed the meal, or at least attempted to.

The Cathedral of Santiago is located in Santiago de Compestella, which rests in the region of Galicia. Galicia is my favorite part of the whole Camino. It is filled with rolling green scenery and stretches all the way to the ocean, where it offers you rugged coastlines—and incredible food. So, by the time I entered the region, I was tired of, as Roshelle rightly described them, the "utilitarian" meals from The Pilgrim Menu and was ready for something tasty.

I remembered from my first Camino that Galicia had some seriously amazing seafood. The dish that really struck me was pulpo, octopus, lightly salted and served up on a platter with nothing else. It was amazing.

I love good food. I love pulpo. I love trekking through Galicia.

Even though Galicia offered me some great food, I was coming to the end of the Camino and I wasn't planning to stop at the Cathedral of Santiago. Rather, I wanted to go to Finisterre. Because it is on the coast and you see nothing but endless ocean on the horizon, it was once thought to be the end of the world. I missed it on the first Camino and thought it would be a fitting and gorgeous place to end my second journey.

However, I had walked for weeks with a group of people who had become my second "Camino Family," and the three-day walk required to make it to Finisterre was more than a lot of them wanted to take on. In fact, no one else wanted to do it, so they weren't in a hurry to get to Santiago and preferred to take some easier, shorter days leading up to the end of the trip.

That meant I couldn't walk into Santiago de Compestella with my "Camino Family" and still make it to the end of the world. I had to choose: do I walk with my friends and embrace community, or do I accomplish my goal and embrace achievement?

Really, the question I had to ask myself was, "What do I love?"

I had asked that question to so many people along the way and had often thought about it a lot myself, too. I came up with a lot of things that I love (recall my list for Chef), but now I was faced with a choice between two things I loved: people and accomplishment. Which way was I going to go?

I told Hannah before I left that nothing was going to stop me from getting to Finisterre. "I'm gonna do it this time, or I'll regret it for the rest of my life," I told her without a single bit of doubt.

I was sure of it. I made plans. I accomplished goals. One time a person described my church as "a bunch of people who get shit done."

Vulgar? Yes—but that didn't make it any less true. I've always thought it was one of the best compliments anyone had ever given me about my church.

The answer was simple. Go to Finisterre.

But I knew it was the wrong answer.

I knew it because I told my daughters the right answer over and over. People are more important than things. I tell them that basically every day. It's how my wife and I teach them to share. Teaching a kid to share is no easy task because we're all radically selfish beings. Heck, adults don't want to share, much less children. I mean, what's the motivation? I'm gonna give up what I want for the sake of someone else's desire—why? That's why telling a child to share just for the sake of sharing doesn't work. You have to give them a framework for understanding why they should share.

People are more important than things.

They're also more important than achieving my goals. Sure, I could walk to Finisterre, but that meant trekking ahead of my "Camino Family" so I'd have the extra three days to do it—and then I'd be doing it all alone. That isn't really a problem for me, but then I'd end up standing and looking at the ocean by myself. I'd experience the satisfaction of "making it" for a moment, and then, that feeling would fade away. Was I willing to set aside my community for that a fleeting (and lonely) moment of accomplishment?

To be honest, yeah.

That's exactly what I wanted to do—but I knew I had to lay it down. I knew that, for me, sacrificing that goal meant more than reaching the ocean.

I didn't fully accept that, however, until I talked to Sarah.

Sarah was really interesting to me. Like Chef and Kelly, she was quick-witted and sarcastic. She probably drank a little too much, but hey, she was on holiday walking through Spain. I could always spot her on the trail, or in a town, because she was tall with dirty blonde hair and usually had her headphones in listening to a music track from a movie. She and Kelly were two peas in a pod.

One of things Kelly had realized about herself on the Camino was that she hated walking. It just wasn't her thing, which was problematic because she was in the middle of a 500-mile trek. So, Kelly found ways to keep herself going. Sometimes she'd spend an extra day in a city and then taxi to meet us. Other times she took a bus, and once, she even rode a bike—which she discovered she didn't like, either. One thing I knew about Kelly, though, was that she'd enjoy walking if she was engaged in a good conversation. That meant I often saw Kelly with Sarah, gabbing away.

Sitting one afternoon at an albergue in a town too small to remember, I watched for Kelly and Sarah to arrive. When they were a few miles out, Kelly texted me. "Keep an eye out for us because we don't really know where you are," it read. The tiny town only had two albergues and they both sat on the main road. I figured there was no way I could miss them.

Then another message came. "Were here, but we can't find you guys."

What the heck, I thought. How did they get past me?

My phone dinged. "I think we're on the wrong side of town. Can you meet us?"

"On my way," I punched in, downing the last of my Americano.

When I found the duo, they were wearing sandals and laughing, and looked like they hadn't walked a single mile all day.

Which was true.

Turned out Kelly and Sarah had slept in really late that morning, and when they ran into one another getting ready, they decided walking was not in the cards for them. Instead, they chose to go to McDonald's.

As you'd imagine, Spain does not have a ton of McDonald's, but that didn't deter Kelly and Sarah. They had a taxi drive them all over the place until they located one, and when they found the object of their fast-food desire, they ordered their food. A ton of it: burgers, fries, you name it. "It was amazing," Kelly told me with complete satisfaction on her face.

Then Kelly and Sarah decided to get a tattoo. Getting Camino tattoos is something more than a few pilgrims do. It's like a badge to remind them of the amazing journey they completed, the friends they met, and the struggles they conquered. The most common Camino tattoos are a shell, an arrow, or the outline of a pilgrim walking. The day after I reached Santiago on my first pilgrimage, I got my Camino tattoo on the top of my right foot: a shell with Saint James' Cross at the center. The decision to do it the day after was probably not the smartest, having my already-sore foot stabbed a thousand times a second by a tattoo needle, but I don't regret it. Like me, people usually get a Camino tattoo after they're done walking. Not Kelly and Sarah. They thought McDonald's and a tattoo was exactly how they wanted to spend their day.

That's not at all how I'd want to spend a day on the Camino, but it made sense for Sarah and Kelly. When I thought about it, I asked myself, "How could I not assume they were gonna do that?" But something about it bothered me. After all, they took an entire day and didn't log a single mile. Nothing. They just randomly decided to forego walking to spend the day together. But obviously, they'd had fun and had no regrets.

Well, I'm sure the next day they regretted eating all that McDonalds.

When I finished walking them back to the albergue, Sarah sat outside with me and got a glass of wine. She offered to buy me a scotch, and I figured it was the perfect time to talk to her about my end-of-the-Camino dilemma.

"So, here's the thing," I said after I complimented her tattoo. "I really want to go to Finisterre, but I also really want to walk with our group."

"What's so special about Finisterre?" she said nonchalantly, lighting a cigarette.

"Well, I didn't get to walk there the first time, and I regretted it a lot."

She looked me straight in the eye and said, "I took a taxi today so that I could walk with you guys tomorrow. You might regret not having gone to Finisterre on your first Camino, but you'll regret leaving us even more."

I wasn't expecting that. I leaned back and took a deep breath. It was almost as though Sarah was reprimanding me.

"The Camino is about relationships," she continued, "You'll regret losing the relationships."

I sat there in silence for a second or two and realized she was correct. I had known it the whole time. I just didn't want to accept it.

I needed someone to tell me what I already knew. Someone like Sarah.

"You're right," I replied, feeling the weight of my dilemma shrink away. "I'm not going to Finisterre. Thanks for the help."

"Whoa, don't blame that on me!" she said with a smile.

Sometimes we just need a little nudge to do the right thing.

Sometimes someone needs to remind us that people are more important than things.

Pilgrims who trek the last 100 kilometers (62 miles) of the Camino de Santiago receive a Compostela, an official certificate from the Catholic Church. This final stretch of the journey starts in a city called Sarria, which happens to be one of the most populous cities along the French Way. Walking through Sarria can be a jolting experience. It's crowded with pilgrims clamoring to organize themselves, and in the alleyways and outskirts are tons of graffiti demeaning the pilgrims who choose to only walk the last 100 kilometers from Sarria to Santiago de Compestella. It compares "real" pilgrims (the ones who have walked the entire 30-day journey) with "fake" pilgrims who do the shorter, seven-day trek.

Although some pilgrims made a big deal about what makes a "real" or "fake" pilgrim, I preferred to compare what I called the "established" pilgrim to the "new" one, and the differences were huge.

Pilgrims walking the entire Camino have already logged over 400 miles by the time they get to Sarria. They've already asked and answered all of the questions about where to sleep, eat, and how to find water. They've established their daily rhythms, from exactly how to unpack each item to the very first thing to do when they get to the next town. These established pilgrims' feet are calloused and don't really ache anymore, their muscles are strong, and their skin is tan. They walk calmly, spend a lot of time in silence, and carry a worn, scuffed pack. They are confident about each day's walk because they already know the trek. They've spent time with it, fought with it, and laughed and cried with it. For them, the trail is no longer a pathway, but it has a personality and a sense of being.

The new pilgrim who starts at Sarria does so like a child, worried about the basic necessities of Camino life. Where are they going to sleep? Will there be enough beds? What about food and water? They wonder how to care for blisters and sore muscles. Their questions are endless and, for the most part, they are loud. They laugh loud, talk loud, and their boots even crunch loud on the trail. They're everywhere, and they make Sarria a place where the "new" and the "experienced" clash, not violently or even in an outspoken manner, but enough to make an experienced pilgrim frustrated and easily annoyed at the newbies on the path.

I remember something happening in me when I walked through Sarria on my second Camino and saw all the pilgrims with their clean boots and shiny new packs. I looked down on them. I felt they hadn't experienced what I had, not from just one but from two Caminos. I knew what it was to be a pilgrim while they didn't have the slightest clue. You're complaining about blisters? Seriously? I solved that ages ago. Just be quiet and walk.

I decided I was better than the new pilgrims because I had experienced more. Because I had experienced more, I knew more. Because I knew more, I was a better pilgrim. A "real" pilgrim. I was what they should aspire to be.

I was so arrogant. But was that because something happened in me— or was something already in me that the presence of the new pilgrims brought to light?

Omar was a newbie, tall and thin with black hair and a huge smile. He started in Sarria and spent a few hours walking with me as I left the city. I could tell he was new because I had walked behind him for a half an hour as he swerved all over the path, flailing his arms around excitedly like he was being attacked by a swarm of gnats as he talked to the other pilgrims. Secretly, I hoped I could pass him by without a word and be on my way.

That didn't happen. No one got past Omar.

He was the kind of guy who exuded joy. He was excited—to be walking, to be outdoors, to be in Spain, and, most of all, to be meeting people. He immediately engaged me as I vainly tried to slide by him. When he found out I was a pastor, it blew his mind.

"But you have tattoos" he said, almost stopping in his tracks. Almost. "And you have a beard. You don't look like a pastor."

"Where I come from," I explained, "it's not uncommon." A smirk crossed my face. I love when people are freaked out that I'm a pastor.

"No pastor I've ever known has tattoos," he replied, staring at my left arm which is basically covered with them.

"So, how many pastors do you know?" It's an important question to ask, especially when speaking with someone from outside the United States. Many non-Americans have their idea of what a pastor is or should be, and it's usually a stuffy old white guy with no sense of humor.

"I don't know," Omar said. "I guess not too many. I don't really know any pastors. I'm not super religious, so that's probably why."

"Why aren't you religious?" I asked, hoping to make him think about religion for a second. Most people are never asked why they aren't religious. If they are, they usually come up with reasons why they shouldn't be. Why they aren't and why they shouldn't be are two very different things.

"It doesn't make sense to me. Why should I be?" he quickly countered as if he'd had the conversation more than a few times before.

He continued, "If I was going to be religious, I would follow Allah, like my dad. So many people blindly believe things without thinking about why they believe them. My dad, though, he thinks about these things. He always has an answer."

Dads are more important than they realize. Dads are demigods.

I then found out it was Omar's dad who suggested he do the Camino de Santiago. Omar's aunt had lived in Santiago but had recently passed away. Omar couldn't attend the funeral because he was working on a cruise ship that was out to sea. He was devastated, so his dad suggested that he walk the Camino, but instead of stopping at the cathedral, he should carry on until he reached his aunt's grave.

So, Omar, with only a week of time off, walked the Camino starting in Sarria. He'd finish in a cemetery where he'd say goodbye to his aunt.

I had a hard time reconciling how Omar could be so joyful while he was walking to a graveyard. I figured it would be rude to ask, but then, assuming he'd told this story a bunch of times already, I decided to find out.

"How can you be so happy when you're walking to mourn your aunt?" I asked hesitantly. I expected him to get angry at me.

He didn't, though. "My aunt walked the Way," he said, a hint of regret in his voice. "She had done it and was constantly telling me how I should do it. I should have done it sooner, while she was alive. I could have walked it and finished on her doorstep. That would have been a Camino! But I'm happy because I know she would be, too, if she knew I was here."

Omar's words hit me like someone had just punched my soul. Here I was, strutting around like I was the aspiration of what a pilgrim should be—and I discover this newbie who was walking to the grave of his aunt. He walked joyfully, in tribute, a pilgrim for the sake of love.

I wasn't a better pilgrim. I was an idiot.

He was a "real" pilgrim. I was a newly humbled one.

Omar reminded me that what matters for the pilgrim is walking, one step in front of the other. It doesn't matter where the pilgrim starts, just that he or she is making the journey.

The last 100 kilometers doesn't just bring new pilgrims, though, but a whole new feeling of excitement. By the time I had walked through Sarria, it was easy for me to cover 20 miles a day, which meant I was going to make it to Santiago in four days. That's nothing when you've already knocked out the first 26. I started to think about what it was going to be like to finally make it into the town square, put down my pack, and take off my boots for the last time. I could feel the anticipation welling up in my stomach. I noticed it in my quickened pace as I thought, I'm actually gonna finish this thing.

I remembered feeling the same way the first time I made the pilgrimage, and I was a little surprised that the feeling returned this time around. It wasn't so much the excitement itself; I'm always excited when I'm about to accomplish a goal. It was somehow more nuanced than that. Something I didn't fully understand yet.

Until the next to last day of my trek provided the perfect explanation.

The walk from Melide to Santa Irene was relatively easy, with a slow descent and diverse terrain composed of dirt trails, roadways, and, at one point, a stream I crossed by hopping from one large rock to the next. With a slight breeze and clear skies, it was a perfect day to hike and think—but my left knee was starting to bother me even though I was wearing my knee brace. At first, it was annoying, but hey, pain is part of the Camino. After a few hours, though, I was being jolted every time my left foot hit the ground. My nerves were sending shockwaves that harshly reminded me I wasn't invincible, even if I thought I was.

Instead of stopping, resting my knee, and taking some ibuprofen like a normal human being, I tried to fight through it. I'd embrace the discomfort, lean on my staff a bit more, and forge on. I was not about to let a little pain stop me from walking and thinking.

By the time my knee was throbbing so bad I could no longer walk or think, I gave in, hobbling into a café that doubled as an albergue and promptly ordering a Jack and Coke. Beverage in hand, I walked through the doorway onto the back patio to find I was alone in the courtyard. It had a koi pond in the middle surrounded by grass running into a vine-covered fence, and tables and chairs were scattered across the back porch. The whole scene seemed perfect for some thoughtful meditation while I nursed my knee.

Why am I so looking forward to getting to Santiago?

Sipping the Jack and Coke, I took off my boots and socks, reclined in the chair, and attempted to clear my mind. But my sore knee brought to mind Ecclesiastes 12, which opens with a description of what it's like to get old, using terms like "the strong man is bent," "the grinders cease," and "those who look through the windows are dimmed." It was sobering to consider getting slow and weak, teeth decaying, eyesight fading, strength leaving. It's all inevitable. There was nothing I could do about it. Eventually, all of us will die, be burned or dropped in a hole, and then be forgotten in a generation or two.

The Jack and Coke was pretty strong.

My sad rumination was briefly distracted by the arrival of a couple who were obviously very much in love. I think they were speaking Italian, but they spoke it in that tone people who have just fallen in love use, like an excited whisper, as they touched each other's arms and caressed one another's hands. It was cute.

As much as I wanted to return to my thoughts (I was certain they were going somewhere significant), when they started talking more urgently in English, I couldn't help but eavesdrop. Suddenly, the girl abruptly stood up, knocking her chair over in the process, and yelled at the man. He leaned back, lifted his chin, and said something in staccato Italian that must have been very insulting because she threw up her arms and stomped off.

Shocked, I stared at the man, wondering what had happened, until he looked right at me. I took that as my cue to get up and leave.

I downed the rest of my Jack and Coke, put on my socks and boots, and limped back out onto the trail. I almost ran into Kelly, who I assumed was still far behind me.

"Hey, Nick!" she said, obviously relieved. "Man, am I glad to see someone I know. I hate today, and I have to pee."

With that, as she scurried past me to the restroom, I suddenly understood why I couldn't wait to get to the end of the journey.

I had started my second Camino assuming that I was going to make it to Santiago, and why not? I'd done it before. I was more prepared than most. It never entered my mind that I wasn't going to finish.

But it should've. I live in a realm of false security. I believe that I can control what will happen, how it will happen, and when it will happen. But that's all just a lie I tell myself so that I feel sure enough to keep moving forward. The truth is I have absolutely no control over anything. I can't guarantee squat. Clearly, I couldn't even keep my knee from revolting against me and ruining my day. So how audacious it was to simply assume I was going to walk all 500 miles of the Camino and know I was going to make it to the end?

Every day, we get out of bed and decide that we know how the day is going to turn out, what's going to happen, and choose to live in the security of that knowledge. But it's a lie. We can't promise anything. We have absolutely no control. We just think we do.

The way the day had gone was stark evidence. I thought I knew what was going to happen, and yet my bad knee betrayed me, the fighting couple shocked me, Kelly surprised me, and according to Ecclesiastes I couldn't even avoid the inevitable decay of my body.

I wasn't excited about getting to Santiago. I was relieved.

I was also grateful—because even though I lived in a world I couldn't control, I was still moving forward in the midst of the chaos. I was still putting one foot in front of the other in the hope I'd cross the finish line. I was just one day away from doing exactly that—and that was not just exciting. It was more—much more.

Kelly came out of the restroom. "How did I catch up to you?"

"My knee really hurts today," I said, trying to shirk it off.

"Have you taken any ibuprofen?" she asked as she hoisted her pack back on.

"No, I haven't taken any the whole trip," I said, feeling kind of proud of myself.

She glared at me. "That's dumb."

I smiled. "Good point," I said, and I put my pack down to find a pain killer.

At least that's one thing I can control.

Walking in Santiago can be confusing. The city is big, bustling with life, and filled with traffic. People swarm the sidewalks trying to go about their daily business as pilgrims wind their way through the crowds. The route to the Cathedral of Santiago is not a straight one at all, ' meanders across busy intersections, down twisting streets, and r and historic buildings alike. The route is marked by brass she' the sidewalk concrete, and they can be easily missed if y attention. I met one lady who had spent an entire day right way, which didn't make a ton of sense becau phone and could look up directions. Google Maps c

The bewildering bustle of the city, though, pa' what I felt when I first arrived in Santiago. There' coming to the completion of a hard task that kind of euphoric. The experience of the Can it any work project I'd ever attempted, even the However, my excitement and relief were ten t. The deep sadness. Because it was my second C was like to finish it. I also knew how it f first Camino wanting, needing, to walk.

idea of walking consumed me like an addiction, and yet I knew it was over.

Now, here I was, in Santiago, and the pilgrim part of me was done. My journey was complete. It was time to break the addiction.

I experienced the exhilaration of the culmination of the Camino while realizing that it was indeed over. It was a loss, and that made me sad.

I can't tell you how many pilgrims I've met since then who long to be back on the trail. They think about it almost every day, and they have committed themselves to doing it over and over again, far more often than my pair of treks.

So, how do you walk when you really want to make it to the end but really don't want it to end at all? The same as you did every other day— but your feet feel a little heavier, each mile seems to take a bit longer, and your mind is muddled to the point you find yourself bogging down.

Jerk. Stall. Repeat.

Roshelle, Kelly, and I met by chance at a café just outside of the city, so we completed the rest of the journey together. I couldn't help but think about Bridget, Dan, and Tabitha, each of them going their own way, each one knowing their journey had to take a different route. Tabitha ended up with some pretty severe blistering and chose to head to Tucson rather than risk infection. Bridget was on a timeline since was traveling after the Camino and we were moving too slowly for she opted to bus past the Meseta and us to Santiago by a few days. Dan could only travel for two weeks, he stopped at Burgos g home.

've been nice to walk to the cathedral with them. But that's urney: recognizing that not everyone has the same Camino, as your journey designed for you. It needs to be different se's.

much as we wound our way through the city, not or thoughtful reflection as much as it was that we were focused on following the shells, avoiding the cars, and weaving our way through all of the people. I was beginning to get stressed out. Follow the shells, dodge the people, and don't walk too fast. Remember, this is the end.

When I spotted the towers of the cathedral, I left the shells. I knew exactly where I was and where I was going. I remembered walking it with Hannah, and I remembered how much I missed her and the girls. I walked faster. I was suddenly ready to be done, go home, and allow this part of me to be completed—so much so that I had to consciously slow down so that Kelly and Roshelle wouldn't lose me in the crowd.

Entering the Plaza Mayor, we spotted Sarah, Chef, and a few others sitting on the ground in the center of the square. They were drinking wine and beer as they watched the reactions of various pilgrims as they finished their journey. Some were crying. Others shouted for joy. Many instantly dropped their pack and took off their shoes. Most everyone had someone take their photo. We walked briskly up to our friends with shouts, cheers, and hugs. Kelly and Roshelle immediately began chit-chatting among the group, but I wasn't ready to visit just yet. I wanted to go and get my Compostela. I figured my journey wasn't officially over until I had that certificate in my hand.

Looking toward where the pilgrim's office was located during my first Camino, I realized there was no line, which meant they must have moved it. I figured someone in our group must have already gone and asked for its whereabouts.

"Hey guys, where's the pilgrim's office?"

Sarah pointed toward a large alleyway on the opposite corner of the square. "That way," she said, "but the line is really long."

Chef piped in. "I heard it takes like two hours to get through the line. I'm gonna wait until tomorrow so I can get there early before everyone starts to arrive."

I thought about it for a second. "I think I'm going to get mine now," I said, assuming they were exaggerating and would rather sit in the square and drink.

They weren't.

The line was freakishly long and filled with pilgrims excitedly sharing stories, complaining about the wait, and shifting from foot to foot. It's surprising how much your feet hurt when standing in line, even after they have been hardened from a 500-mile trek.

An hour-and-a-half later, I finally shuffled up to the counter. I showed my pilgrims passport to a guy I'm gonna call "Niles" because he seemed like a Niles to me, meaning that I didn't enjoy him at all. (No offense intended if your name is Niles.) Anyway, this guy, Niles, had spent the last 90 minutes sitting in his chair, abruptly shooting his arm into the air and waving it back and forth, then just as abruptly dropping it back down. He didn't say anything to accompany his repeated gesture, at least not that I could hear, but the line had slowly snaked forward.

It wasn't until I was next in line that and I heard him holler out, "Next pilgrim, please," and then sit back down. He sounded annoyed.

At that point, to be completely honest, I was, too. His antics bothered me, my feet were aching, my stomach was growling, and something was telling me Niles was going to be a huge pain in my neck. I leaned my staff up against the counter, pulled out my pilgrim's passport, and handed it to him.

"Didn't you see me wave my arm the first time?" His tone was condescending and pretentious.

I wanted to say, Yes, you lug nut, I saw you wave your scrawny little arm a few hundred times. Think I'm blind or something? Instead, I actually replied, "Sorry. I didn't realize you were calling me over." I tried to say it as calmly and cheerfully as possible, but he said nothing. He just kept staring at my passport as if it was written in Egyptian Sanskrit.

For the longest time we remained that way until Niles, still looking down at my passport, said, "You didn't get two stamps a day the last 100 kilometers."

"What does that mean?" I blurted, and Niles jerked in his chair from my outburst. Truth was, I knew exactly what he meant. I had heard another pilgrim mention that we needed to get two stamps a day the last 100K or else we wouldn't be recognized as completing the walk. She had said something about people faking the pilgrimage, which I had completely disregarded because it made no sense to me that anyone would pretend to walk the Camino just to get a piece of paper. So, I just continued to get a single stamp a day like I had on my first pilgrimage.

I should have listened.

"Well, you were supposed to get two stamps every day that you walked the last 100 kilometers," he said patronizingly, leaning back in his chair and looking over his glasses at me as though I were a mere mortal cowering in the presence of a deity.

This guy might actually refuse to give me my Compostela, I thought, and anger seared through me.

What you do when you are angry is really important. My first thought was to demand Niles give it to me, figuring that if I yelled and intimidated him, it'd take him down a notch or ten and he'd just hand it over. But that would have been wrong. My second thought was to humbly beseech him for my Compostela. Perhaps that would appeal to his self-appointed transcendency and result in him giving it to me as an act of mercy upon my pitiful soul. But I needed to own the fact that I had messed up by not taking the stamp requirement seriously.

I took a deep breath. "Oh, I didn't realize that I needed to do that," I said, voice level and calm. "I mean, I had heard people talking about it, but I didn't know, and, you know, people say a lot of things that aren't true." I was babbling, but I was exhausted, and I really wanted my piece of paper.

"I'm not sure if I can give you the Compostela," he declared, stone cold. Clearly, my babble wasn't convincing him.

I decided to take a different approach. "I didn't see anything posted saying we needed two stamps."

"It's not a hard thing to do," he shot back. "You get one where you take a break, and you get one at the albergue you stay at."

My heart pounded. "Well, I didn't know I needed to do that," I replied, stifling a sigh. "I would have definitely done it if I knew I was supposed to."

He looked down again at the passport. "There are stamps from the whole pilgrimage," I pointed out, my tone bordering on whining. "Can't you overlook the lack of the missing stamps?"

"Okay," his said, his voice showing no emotion.

I could hardly believe my ears. "Okay?" I asked

"I said okay!" he proclaimed as if he were Zeus ready to fling a lightning bolt.

"Okay!" I repeated excitedly. I could feel the anger and worry begin to fade away from me.

He pointed at a certificate on his desk. "Here's your Compostela. I just need to record it." Niles then took my name and some other information, wrote it down, and handed me a signed Compostela.

"Next time," he said, "get two stamps." With that, I was dismissed.

As I began walking back to the square, conflict rose within me. Why didn't Niles just give me the certificate in the first place? I mean, he must have had a ton of pilgrims without double stamps for the last 100K. Was that whole thing just a power play? Did he know that he was going to give me the Compestela the whole time?

I was starting to get frustrated again until I realized something very simple. It didn't matter. My Compostela was in my hand. My journey was officially over.

When I made it back to the group, I was offered a beer and a spot to sit—but only after they mocked me for having to get my Compestela right away. So, I sat, drank my beer, and took in the victory of completing the walk. I did that for about an hour until my butt started to hurt. Apparently, God had not designed my body to sit on cement. Besides, I was getting bored.

"Hey guys, I'm gonna go explore the city," I said, standing up,

"Anyone want to join me?"

Kelly was laying on her back with her head resting on her pack. She looked at me like I was insane. "You wanna walk around right now?"

"Heck, yeah!" I replied. "There's a ton of stuff to check out!" Despite my enthusiasm, I could tell no one else was going to come with me.

Then Roshelle jumped up. "I'm gonna check in to my Airbnb."

"I would rather lay here and relax," Kelly said, fluffing her pack, "I've walked enough."

The rest of the group nodded in agreement but offered to watch my pack, so I didn't have to drag it around the city. I thanked them, and Roshelle and I headed into town.

I meandered around for a few hours while Roshelle went to the Airbnb, and when we returned, they were all still there in the middle of the square, sitting on the ground.

That became the routine for the next two days. Roshelle and I would yo-yo back and forth from the square into the city and back again to find everyone lounging in the square.

After a while, it made me wonder, Why lay around in the square? It wasn't just my friends who were doing it. Most everyone else was, too. Why? I decided to ask Chef. "What else am I going to do?" was his reply. That didn't satisfy my curiosity at all, so I decided to query a few more pilgrims, and they all basically said the same thing.

"What else am I going to do?"

It was a month or so later, back home in Tucson, before I realized the importance of that question.

For the pilgrim walking the Camino de Santiago, the journey is like an entire life lived in a single month. You start out knowing nothing, thinking only of your basic needs of water, food, and shelter. You start as an infant. Then you figure out where to find the necessities and your body gets stronger. You begin forming relationships. You're growing.

Eventually, you form a routine, your liturgy, and continue working out the practicalities of the Camino. Your relationships deepen as you become known and begin to know others. Bonds form, and you start discussing the important things of life such as, "What do you love?" You begin applying lessons you've learned. You're maturing—just in time to face the mid-life crises, the Mesetas along the way. The relationships aren't as interesting, the views aren't as exciting, and you find yourself trudging through the journey, longing for something, anything, to change. This is where some people spin out of control and leave, whether they have a good reason for it or not. Others distract themselves to offset the boredom, and some learn something more about themselves, spend their time reflecting, and ultimately discover a purpose, desire, or reality they never considered before. Mid-life crises are different for everyone.

The last 100 kilometers represent your older years, and you walk with a wealth of Camino wisdom. You've been on the journey longer than most, you aren't worried or loud, and you journey in peace. You have a lot to offer new pilgrims if you choose, or you dismiss them, annoyed by the ruckus they cause. Sometimes you can learn from them, gaining a fresh perspective about the long journey you're about to complete.

Then you enter Santiago. What happens when you've grown old and reach the finish line? For many, walking into the Cathedral of Santiago is the death of their pilgrim selves. Even more than that, the Pilgrims Mass signifies the end for each sojourner. You watch the "botafumeiro" swing across the cathedral as the nuns sing. You hear the priest speak Scripture over you, remembering your journey as the smell of incense wafts through the sanctuary. It is a funeral—a beautiful funeral for your pilgrim self that you actually get to experience.

Near the end of the Way, the signs declare, "Santiago isn't the end." They're right, to an extent. The journey continues on. Life goes on. You will have more adventures, trials, and pilgrimages of various kinds. Hopefully, you leave Santiago with a new perspective, but your pilgrim identity is definitely left in that Cathedral.

So, the question you must ask yourself is, "What else am I going to do?"

Or, more specifically, "How do I walk now—knowing there will be another funeral someday at the end of my life's journey?"

"And the life I now live in the flesh I live by faith in the Son of God, who loved me and gave himself for me."

(Galatians 2:20)

Made in the USA
San Bernardino, CA
23 July 2020

75873051R00080